The Waiting Room

Copyright © 2019 by Caroline Klug
Personal Message © 2019 by Caroline Klug

All rights reserved. No part of this publication may be reproduced, distributed, or transmitted in any form or by any means, including photocopying, recording, or other electronic or mechanical methods, without the prior written permission of the author, except in the case of brief quotations embodied in critical reviews and certain other noncommercial uses permitted by copyright law. For permission requests, contact the author using the Contact page on www.CarolineKlug.com. Please be sure to include "Permission Request" in the Subject line.

All Scriptures are taken from the Holy Bible, New International Version®, NIV®. Copyright © 1973, 1978, 1984, 2011 from Biblica, Inc.® Used with permission.

All definitions, unless otherwise indicated, are used with permission from the Merriam-Webster Dictionary; Merriam-Webster.com. 2019. https://www.merriam-webster.com (May 2019).

All Hebrew and Greek root words, unless otherwise indicated, are taken from Vine, W. E., Merrill F. Unger, William White, and W. E. Vine. 1985. Vine's complete expository dictionary of Old and New Testament words. Nashville: Nelson.

Cover design by Tim Fitzpatrick
Author photograph by James Klug

To request Caroline Klug for a speaking event or appearance, please contact the author using the Contact page on www.CarolineKlug.com. Please be sure to include "Event Request" in the Subject line.

ISBN: 978-1-7339008-2-9 (eBook)
ISBN: 978-1-7339008-3-6 (paperback)
ISBN: 978-1-7339008-5-0 (paperback)

Printed in the United States of America

The Waiting Room

When You're on Your Knees Struggling to Believe

Caroline Klug

Contents

A Personal Message 8

First Things First 10

Step 1: Remind Your Heart 14
    Remind | Labor Pains 20
    Remind | Impatience 24
    Remind | The Wait (Part 1) 30
    Remind | The Wait (Part 2) 34
    Remind | When, God, When? 38
    Remind | Where the Air is Clear 42
    Remind | War of Wills 46
    Remind | Walk by Faith 50
    Remind | The Peace of God 54
    Remind | Milk and Honey 58

Step 2: Release Your Heart 62
    Release | Letting Go 68
    Release | A New Thing (Part 1) 72
    Release | A New Thing (Part 2) 76
    Release | Lift Up Your Eyes 80
    Release | Spring of Life (Part 1) 84
    Release | Spring of Life (Part 2) 88

Release | The Call to Persevere 92

Release | The Climb Upward....................96

Release | Surrender 100

Release | Cut the Ropes 104

Step 3: Revive Your Heart...........................110

Revive | Moving Mountains 116

Revive | Great Expectations 120

Revive | Dry Bones (Part 1) 124

Revive | Dry Bones (Part 2) 128

Revive | Let Nothing Move You 132

Revive | Set Your Mind...........................136

Revive | Be Watchful 140

Revive | The Upper Room.......................144

Revive | Suddenly....................................148

Revive | Ten Years 152

Parting Thoughts..158

Scripture References....................................162

This book is dedicated to my amazing husband, Jim, who happens to be a promise I waited a decade for.

Jim – the waiting room was cold, the chairs were hard, and there was no coffee. But now that my name has been called, and God has put my hand in yours, it's been worth every second of that wait. I'm so blessed to have you, and can't wait to see all the ways God will continue to use our partnership. I love you more.

~ C.K.

A Personal Message

Greetings, Loved One. I'm so glad you're here. I want you to know I'm praying for you. Yes, *you*. I may not know you by name, and I may not know your exact situation, but I'm praying over every person who finds this book in their hands. My prayer is that God would rain down His blessings over your petitions, and give you comfort in the wait.

Now that you're here, let's start with a prayer.

Dear Father, I pray You will use this time to remind my heart who You are. Give me eyes to see, ears to hear, and a heart to understand the amazing things You have planned for me. Create in me a spirit of hope and a faith that endures. Give me a heart filled with expectation. Let my steadfast trust honor You and bring encouragement to the people around me. Thank You in advance for all You're going to do in me, for me, and through me. Amen.

He's listening. He's been listening the whole time. Your God doesn't sleep or slumber (Psalm 121:4). He knows you intimately, and He knows every thought you have before you speak even one of them (Psalm 139:4). Trust and have faith. Let God turn your unexpected into the expected.

Be blessed,
C.K.

Caroline Klug

First Things First

If you're in need of a miracle, interceding for a loved one, or believing in God to move a mountain, getting on your knees is the easy part. The hard part is waiting. Not seeing the answers we long for can leave us feeling depressed, and even doubtful. We begin fixing our eyes on the world around us, rather than the One who made the world.

If this is you, don't lose heart. I pray our time together can help lift your eyes and encourage your heart. To do this, our journey is laid out into three steps:

Step 1: *Remind* Your Heart
Step 2: *Release* Your Heart
Step 3: *Revive* Your Heart

As you move through this book, each section is designed to remind you of some very important perspectives during your wait, help you release all the things you've been holding on to into God's care, and revive your heart with an infusion of faith that can move mountains.

Before you jump in, I'd like to give you a few practical suggestions in order to get the most out of each of these sections.

Align with Him
Make sure what you're praying for is from God and is scripturally sound. If it is, you can approach the Throne with confidence. If it isn't, I'd encourage you to bring the spirit of what you're asking for before God and let Him help you transform it into something that is.

For example, praying to win the lottery might not line up very well with Scripture. Perhaps at the heart of your prayer is fear over your financial situation. Bring that fear to God instead. Ask Him to help you be a good steward with money and tithing, pay off your debts, and prosper in whatever way He knows is best.

Expect Him
Come to God with an expectant heart. I believe few things would honor God more in your prayer life than coming with a heart that beats with wild excitement for the unimaginable things you know He's capable of. It's proclaiming your faith before a single word of your request falls from your lips.

If you're unsure or struggling with this, spend time in His Word and learn more about His character and capabilities. Read about how Abraham and Sarah conceived a child at ages 100 and 90, respectively, to fulfill the promise of descendants (Genesis 15, 21). Read about how Moses parted the Red Sea to help the Israelites escape death and persecution (Exodus 16) and all the amazing miracles along the way, until Joshua led them into their Promised Land (Joshua 1). Read about how Daniel's friends, Shadrach, Meshach, and Abednego, were delivered from the fiery furnace (Daniel 3) or how

The Waiting Room

Daniel himself was protected when thrown into the lion's den (Daniel 6).

I could go on and on. The important thing to note is the same God who performed all these miracles is the same God you serve today and is working on your promise (Hebrews 13:8).

Praise Him

Don't forget to praise Him through your storm. No matter what your circumstance, God is on the Throne and is worthy of all our praise. Acknowledge who He is and make Him a priority over your need.

One of the stories in the Bible I find utterly spectacular is when God helped Jehoshaphat and Judah's army defeat two armies who came to wage war against them (2 Chronicles 20). God told Jehoshaphat this battle was His and although a vast army was coming against them, instructed Jehoshaphat to send praise and worshipers as his army's front line. Can you imagine how frightened Jehoshaphat must have been? If we look at that with our earthly eyes, you'd think those poor people singing and worshipping, with nothing to protect themselves, were being sent to the slaughter. But Jehoshaphat trusted God. What happened next raises the hair on my arms. As the front lines sang and worshiped God, God threw the two enemy armies into confusion until the enemies annihilated themselves. I hope this screams encouragement to you and reminds you of the power of praise.

You've got this. But more importantly, *He's* got this. Whether it's been a day or a decade, don't lose hope. You serve a mighty God, capable of doing immeasurably more than you could ever ask or imagine (Ephesians 3:20). God has a plan for your life, and His timing is always perfect.

God loves you and He is for you. Let's get to it, shall we?

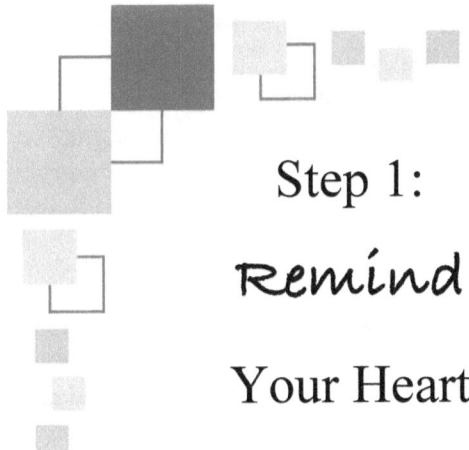

Step 1:
Remind
Your Heart

Being on your knees and sending your prayers up to the Father of the heavenly lights is the most important thing you can be doing. But let's be real. It's hard. Especially when it's for people or situations near and dear to our hearts. I know firsthand how it feels to be praying fervently for something and watching it unfold in the complete opposite direction. Not only is that crushing to see, but it threatens to deflate our faith like air from a blown tire. When those things happen, you've got to decide to see with spiritual eyes rather than earthly eyes. You have to get out your patch kit, plug the hole that's leaking faith, and keep moving forward. That means you keep getting on your knees and resolve to keep bringing your requests to God, despite what your earthly circumstances are telling you.

    I know I just made that sound easy, but I also know the reality that it can be a daily struggle. The writings in this book were born out of some of my personal struggles, so I want to take a moment to appreciate and acknowledge wherever you're at.

So, how do we move past these emotions? This first step is all about reminding our hearts of some very important things that give us the right perspective while we're in the waiting room. Let's look at a few of those.

There is an Order to Things

God's vantage point is well beyond ours. If you see the trees, He sees the planet. If you see the planet, He sees the galaxies. There isn't anything that escapes His view, and there is no element of anything that exists – past, present, or future – that He doesn't consider. God operates in an entirely different dimension than we do. In His world, there is no dimension of time or space. It's all fluid and He sees beyond the boundaries in which we tend to think.

You and I may have trouble grasping all of that, and although we may feel uncomfortable, God is perfectly comfortable and supernaturally capable. Because of all He sees and knows, He is uniquely and solely qualified to set the order of things that will maximize the glory for His Kingdom. He knows what you need and when you need it. He knows what *every* person needs and when they need it. All of those things fit together like one, glorious cosmic puzzle, and He drew the picture of that puzzle long before you or I even existed. Trust if God is asking you to wait just a little bit longer, He has a very good reason, and He will give you everything you need to be comfortable and at peace during your wait.

He's a Heart God

It's easy to get wrapped up in the promise we're looking to receive. It becomes our single focus, and obtaining it is the culmination of what we call victory. We have to consider that God's definition of victory might be a little different than ours. What I'm about to say isn't always what we want to hear, but the sooner we grasp it, the sooner (I believe) we can stop wandering around in the desert, like the Israelites did for forty years (Exodus).

The wait is not always about what we're getting, but what God is doing *in* us and who we're *becoming* while we're waiting.

God is much more concerned with who you are than what you have. Don't get me wrong – the things you want could very well be God-given promises having great significance for the Kingdom. But I don't think it's worth as much to God if you are lost in it along the way. God tells us He works all things for the good of those who are called according to His purposes (Romans 8:28). You might be praying for physical healing and miss the opportunity for spiritual or emotional healing along your journey. Think about it this way – if God heals your physical body, you sure would have a great testimony to share the power of Christ with others. But if you're an emotional mess inside as a result of the wait, how powerful will that testimony be for the Kingdom?

Consider this. The promise God wants to bless you with may not rest in what you receive at the end of your wait, but what happens inside of you during it.

Using Spiritual Eyes

Before you can get into a car and drive, you have to learn the rules of the road. Driver's Education class is not just a rite of passage; it's a requirement if you want to pass the test. Driving lessons not only teach us the rules, but how to assess the things happening on the road around us. God uses our journeys in much the same way. He uses them to train our eyes to see things from His perspective rather than the world's.

I have come to both love and hate seeing things that are contradictory to what God speaks to my heart. The hate part is easy. That's the part that messes with our minds and our hearts because what we see doesn't line up to what we're hoping for. The love part is much harder, and takes time to develop. It's the part that challenges us and grows our faith by giving us opportunities to stand firm no matter what might be swirling around our heads. We could be standing in the middle of a full-on tornado and watch our dream get picked up and thrown beyond our field of vision. What we may not see is God relocating our dream to a better spot so it can be all He intends it to be. What kind of a difference could it make for us if instead of crying in defeat, we got excited, knowing God was at work?

Reality is not what we see. It's what God sees.

Go Through the Motions

When it comes to the situations we are praying about, most of the time, the only way to it is through it.

The Waiting Room

As a kid, I used to watch the TV show Star Trek, and marveled at the idea of someday being able to "beam" wherever I wanted to go in a nanosecond (for you science-minded people, that's one billionth of a second). My prayer life used to be like that. If I'm honest, it sometimes still is. I want God to beam me to my final destination, so I don't have to go through all the waiting and wondering. Praying for nanosecond answers may not always be in our best interest. Sometimes God will give us quick answers, but we'd never grow our faith or character if He *always* kept us from the hard parts.

As you take in these next few chapters, let your heart be reminded there is a pre-destined order to all things, there are things God wants to do inside of you to prepare you for your blessing, and He's using this journey to teach you how to see with spiritual eyes. Allow God to take you *through* it in order to get *to* it.

Caroline Klug

Remind | Labor Pains

> I tell you the truth, you will weep and
> mourn while the world rejoices. You will
> grieve, but your grief will turn to joy. A
> woman giving birth to a child has pain because
> her time has come; but when her baby is born
> she forgets the anguish because of her joy
> that a child is born into the world.
> John 16:20-21

Jesus is comforting His disciples in this passage. They've just learned they'll soon be without Him, and they're completely dismayed at the thought. Jesus is helping them understand the glory in His death, and the necessary pain required to birth a joy that is everlasting. You can apply these words as a healing balm to your own suffering heart while experiencing a time of waiting.

There are times when God chooses to deliver us out of a trial or bring an answer very quickly. Can I get an amen? However, there are times God will require us to walk what feels like a very long road. This requires a lot of trust in Him but, let me assure you, God doesn't do anything haphazardly. Stop with me for a moment and think about the fact that every day of your life was written in God's book before one of them came into being (Psalm

139:16). Really digest that concept. Powerful stuff, right? I don't know about you, but my mind gets completely blown when I really try to process the forethought God has on every day of every one of our lives. Our God is a planner, and there is order to everything He does. You can be confident in His forethought of your present situation, and the steps required to bring it to fruition. This brings us to the heart of our time together today.

Within our journey, a crucial developmental process is taking place. Just as a baby in the womb, if we force it out too soon, there are complications, and often, death. The development of a baby in utero is a stunning process. When we recognize the great mysteries and profound complexity of this process, God can use this to teach us an important lesson about waiting for His deliverance. The gestational period of a baby is very exact, and things develop in a very specific and important order. When God speaks something to your heart, He's doing so with the knowledge of what's to come, and exactly how it is to come about. What He requires of you is trust, patience, and obedience. Regardless of moments of fear or disobedience, God ultimately knows what it will take to bring what He has spoken to pass. He knows what He's doing. It may be painful, but I've learned the more painful it becomes, the closer you usually are to your answer.

> **A crucial developmental process is taking place. Just as a baby in the womb, if we force it out too soon, there are complications, and often, death.**

When I was seven months pregnant with my daughter, I was taking the required Lamaze class, in

The Waiting Room

which they help to prepare you physically and mentally for the painful birthing process ahead. The instructor was demonstrating with a plastic baby and skeletal representation of a woman's hips and pelvic bones, how the baby descends and is birthed. All eyes were riveted on the instructor as she placed the baby inside the skeleton and began moving it downward, laughing as the baby got stuck midway through the pelvis. This required her to jam her hand down on it to free it from its position. Nervous laughter turned into several nauseatingly green faces. Other than learning the final stages of dilation are termed "the hurricane hour" for very painful reasons, I don't think I remembered a single word she said after that. My mind was fixated on the terrifying reality this baby had to come out, and it was going to hurt – a lot.

Sometimes we panic when faced with a trial we know is going to hurt. With childbirth, it's a bit easier to come to the realization that we have to go through it in order to receive that bundle of joy into our arms. In life's journeys, it's not always easy to continue walking, because we may not be able to see the joy that lies ahead of us in a tangible form. However, if God promised a blessing, we can be certain it's there in the heavenly realm and waiting for His perfect timing – and looking exactly as He knows is best. It comes down to a question of who you believe God is. It comes down to whether or not you're going to choose to believe what He spoke to your heart. If God is asking you to walk a difficult path, you can trust it's for a very good reason – one He will reveal to you in His timing.

For those of us who have had the honor of birthing a baby, we remember the joy of being told we were pregnant – or for those of us on our journeys, the moment God spoke a promise to our hearts. For nine long months, or whatever the length of your journey, we watch our bodies change and our hearts grow deep with love for a child or a promise we have not yet seen. We spend hours, days, or even years in immeasurable pain and discomfort, until that moment – that beautiful, life-breathing moment – when we are looking our promise in the face. The pain subsides, and all that's left is a battle scar full of stories of triumph.

Just as every day in the womb is a time of growth for new life, as you walk through a time of fiery trial, you can rest assured every step you take is a necessary detail in the growth of your character and the maturing of your faith. I pray you will never lose heart and give up.

Your eyes saw my unformed body; all the days ordained for me were written in Your book before one of them came to be. How precious to me are Your thoughts, God! How vast is the sum of them! Psalm 139:16-17

Remind | Impatience

*Let us hold unswervingly to the hope we
profess, because He who promised is faithful.*
Hebrews 10:23

I hold unswervingly, all right – usually to the constant swirl of thoughts going on in my head at any given moment. It's an ever-constant mental multi-tasking extravaganza. I think Barnum and Bailey would be impressed. I pride myself on my ability to effectively and efficiently get things done when time is a commodity. It's exhausting but satisfying. As much as I view my multi-tasking and drive as a strength, I've come to realize it's also a "watch-out" for something much more dangerous – impatience. How often do we pray for God to move in our lives and then, in our impatience, take it upon ourselves to make something happen?

Last year the power cord for my laptop was missing. I was going through rooms, drawers, and cars looking for it. How could I possibly have misplaced it? We would be leaving in a few days for Albuquerque, New Mexico, to visit with family over Christmas. Without that cord, I couldn't bring my laptop and write while we were there. I knew I had the option of going to Best Buy and dishing out $50 for a new one, but my common sense told me it was somewhere in the house. I prayed for God to uncover where it was. Yes, I prayed over my laptop cord. God cares about the little things (Matthew 10:30). Although we had a few days before leaving, my impatience got the best of me and I went and bought a new one. On my way home from Best Buy, I felt a little convicted. I had only prayed a short while before going to the store. When I got home, I decided I would not open the box and, instead, spend a little more time looking. Within minutes, I found it. It was in our home safe. Don't ask. It's a long story. At least it wasn't the refrigerator.

When we step out ahead of Him, it always costs us – whether it's time or money, or things much worse. Impatience can cause us to compromise our beliefs, settling for something less than what God would have blessed us with in His timing. Unfortunately, I wrote the book on this one. As a single woman, longing for a true partner – a man I could love and respect, who would love and respect me, and with whom I could share a deep faith – I often let my impatience get the better of me, and I spent time in relationships that were not God's best for me. I wasted a lot of time. It wasn't until I set my face like flint (Isaiah 50:7), determined to do this in His way and His timing, that God introduced me to Jim, who is now my husband.

> **Impatience can cause us to compromise our beliefs, settling for something less than what God would have blessed us with in His timing.**

I'm extremely blessed to say Jim is my true partner – the one I spent years praying for. A decade, actually. I'm guessing your left eye just twitched a little when I said decade. You'll read the full story on this later in the

The Waiting Room

book, so I won't spoil it all now. Suffice it to say, there isn't a day that goes by that I don't thank God for him, but I know stepping out ahead of God and His timing cost me a lot of time and unnecessary emotional turmoil. I even find myself wondering sometimes if Jim had to endure waiting while God was waiting for me to get my act together. I try not to put that one through the circus though, as I know God uses all things for good (Romans 8:28).

Settling for something less can also cost others. Our witness is almost always compromised when we're impatient. Irritability and restlessness are two words used to define impatience. Our behavior is rarely kind when we are irritable or restless. I've seen the kindest person turn into a velociraptor while driving or having to wait in a long line. For out of the overflow of the heart the mouth speaks (Luke 6:45). Yikes. If that's the case, we all need a good, long look at our inflated egos and sense of entitlement. Does the person ahead of us who needs a little extra time at the register deserve less service than we do? Does the person in front of us on the highway driving the speed limit deserve the judgment we pour out – mentally or verbally? What if those same people walked into our churches on Sunday morning and saw us? Talk about the happy circus music coming to a screeching halt.

As I like to say, what's the "so what" in all of this? First, as our Scripture at the beginning of the chapter says, He who promised is faithful. Because of that faithfulness, there's something very powerful available to us. Hope. God calls us to believe and to be witnesses to those around us who desperately need to see the light of His love. I understand first-hand how difficult waiting can be for some people. It has a tendency to shine a light on the emptiness one may feel if they are alone, and cause doubt to creep in over wondering if God is still working out their prayers. Don't let the devil get a foothold on you with that kind of thinking, and don't let him use it to create a negative witness to those around you. Have faith in God. Have faith that He's working out all things for your good in His perfect timing. Don't spend time feeling sorry for yourself. Instead, be a light to someone else. If you're feeling lonely, open your home to someone else who might be feeling lonely. Get out and do a good service for someone in need. Visit an elderly person who may be alone. You might be surprised how that changes your perspective and puts the blessing back on your head.

We know the story. We know about the babe born in a manger. We know His name is Jesus and He came to save the world. God loves us so passionately. He not only sent us His Son as Savior for eternity, but as the hope of all who call Him Savior in this world today. There's never a reason for us to be crushed in spirit. "Jesus looked at them and said, 'With man this is impossible, but with God all things are possible'" (Matthew 19:26). Have patience by embracing the hope that is yours through Jesus. King David said it well – "I am still confident of this: I will see the goodness of the Lord in the land of the living" (Psalm 27:13). That land of the living means the here and now. Embrace your Savior and you will embrace what it means to truly live in joy and hope. May you be blessed beyond measure in all the fullness of Him who fills everything in every way (Ephesians 1:23).

The Waiting Room

◼️ Praise be to the God and Father of our Lord Jesus Christ! In His great mercy He has given us new birth into a living hope through the resurrection of Jesus Christ from the dead, and into an inheritance that can never perish, spoil, or fade—kept in Heaven for you, who through faith are shielded by God's power until the coming of the salvation that is ready to be revealed in the last time. *1 Peter 1:3-5*

Caroline Klug

Remind | The Wait (Part 1)

> I wait for the Lord, my whole being waits,
> and in His Word I put my hope.
> Psalm 130:5

I'm convinced I must have been preoccupied, off looking for a Starbucks, when God was handing out patience. While I was ordering a tall, non-fat, no whip, extra hot mocha, someone else was gratefully accepting my portion. I am a weak human, easily tempted.

Unfortunately, we all know it doesn't work that way. Characteristics like patience take time to build. I'm realizing more and more that some take a lifetime to build. The patience I'm talking about is more than what's required to wait in a long line. It's much more demanding of our wills. It's patience in the wait for the promises of God. Fortunately for us, we serve a God whose control is complete and whose timing is perfect. In Part 1, we'll take a look at the wait from our perspective. In Part 2, we will look at it from God's.

We all have desires and promises in our hearts, which we feel are God-given. These promises can look like the blessing of a child, deliverance from an illness, salvation of a loved one, or even a life calling being fulfilled. Regardless of the dream, we typically have to wait for it, and that's where things get sketchy. We live in an age of instant gratification. From our perspective, we ought to be able to download our promise like a song in iTunes. Our ability to cope with the little "processing" icon grows more and more difficult. We know God has His reasons for the processing time required but for us, it can seem excruciating, and cause us to either doubt or run out ahead.

Having to wait for something often means we have a lot of time to think about it, which frequently results in a healthy serving of doubt. We don't always share our dreams with other people because of fear of how they might react, or how they would view us if it didn't pan out the way we say it should. We struggle enough with doubt, and certainly don't need Joe Blow throwing gas on the fire, telling us what was spoken to our heart is a pipe dream, or even impossible. If this is you, I have great news. If your desires and passions are God-given, then, rest assured, they will come to pass if you're obedient in doing what He asks of you. God can place a burning desire on your heart, but you must be the one to believe He will fulfil it, no matter how long the wait. You have to be the one to walk through the doors He opens to get you there.

Maybe you've worked through your fear and are now finding yourself running too far ahead. As God-given as our passion can be, it can also cause us to step out in front of God if it's not balanced with a spirit of patience. We get antsy when things don't happen in our timing, and we move in ways not directed by the Spirit (Galatians 5:16-17). God instructs us to wait on Him, and for a very good reason. Everything which happens is

The Waiting Room

carefully woven together with a spiritual intricacy beyond what we are capable of fathoming. He has a grand design, and our steps are ordered (Proverbs 16:9). If you try to take things into your own hands, you may find that wait getting a little longer.

God calls all of us to dream in relation to our God-given purpose, requiring obedience to Him in order to bring us there. God isn't cruel. He won't press a God-honoring promise on your heart without intention to fulfill it (Ephesians 1:9-10). We can rest in patience as we trust in His timing. It's difficult, and sometimes even painful, to lay our hearts on the table in belief for all to see. We can spend the time necessary in His Word to know who the Promise Maker is, but we are human and we will still walk through times of doubt or weakness. We are creatures of need and must accept the fact we'll fail at times. We may even feel like giving up hope because we just don't see it. Remember this – God will not condemn you for a feeling, but He will watch to see what you do in the face of it.

We are, by nature, impatient, and I think we become afraid of how long God will ask us to wait. Sometimes it's a day and sometimes it can be decades. There's that eye twitch again. Did you know Abraham and Sarah waited 25 years for the fulfilment of God's promise of a child (Genesis 12, 15-17)? Don't get discouraged by that. Not every promise will require a wait that long, but we still

> **God will not condemn you for a feeling, but He will watch to see what you do in the face of it.**

need to embrace the lesson of patience God is providing. It's one of the things God uses to grow us into our best

Caroline Klug

self. Until next time, think on a possible God perspective – the receiving of our blessing may have more to do with what we become during the wait than about the blessing itself.

> ◰ I waited patiently for the Lord; He turned to me and heard my cry. He lifted me out of the slimy pit, out of the mud and mire; He set my feet on a rock and gave me a firm place to stand. He put a new song in my mouth, a hymn of praise to our God. Many will see and fear and put their trust in the Lord. Psalm 140:1-3

Remind | The Wait (Part 2)

> I wait for the Lord, my whole being waits,
> and in His Word I put my hope.
> Psalm 130:5

In Part 1, we talked about the difficulty we experience waiting for the promises God has spoken to our hearts. In our humanness, we see things from a limited perspective and may miss a much bigger picture at hand. Our opportunity is to look at things from God's perspective and in light of who He is. God is all powerful. He has the ability to make anything come to pass. Why then, would there be a reason to delay any God-given promise for even a moment? God continually reminds me He is a *heart* God. You can trust that when God is working, it most assuredly has to do with someone's heart. The receiving

> **The receiving of your blessing may have more to do with how you think and what you become during the wait, than the blessing itself.**

of your blessing may have more to do with how you think and what you become during the wait, than the blessing itself.

Because of our sinful natures, we can be selfish people who continually get distracted by the wants of this world. As our perfect example, Christ came to this earth to lay His life down and become a servant to us. He put aside all of His personal desires and accepted the work of His Father for the joy set before Him (Hebrews 12:2). There are numerous Biblical references to support the fact that God does indeed desire us to be blessed in this life, and to receive the desires of our hearts. However, Christ gave to us the two most important commands – to love God with everything in us (Mark 12:30), and the Great Commission (Matthew 28:18-20) to reach others. In keeping with this we must understand something. What God desires us to receive before and above anything else is Him. What He desires us to do before and above anything else, is to reach His lost. If the things we pray for take on a greater importance in our hearts than Him, God may very well place that on hold until He assumes the rightful priority in our hearts. There is nothing of more significance to God than His relationship with you or the work He calls you to. We need to continually check ourselves to ensure the desires of our hearts are aligning with our God-given purpose.

There are a billion possibilities as to why your promise might not yet have manifested. Those listed above are merely the obvious reasons we all need to be reminded of. What's more difficult are those reasons that are not so obvious. Your heart is very precious to God and He desires only good things for you. Like a father who knows best for his child, so God knows when we're ready to receive. God is much more interested in who you are rather than what you have. If building

> **God is much more interested in who you are rather than what you have.**

The Waiting Room

characteristics in you that honor God means delaying a promise, then that is a decision He will make in the best interest of your heart. Other times, it may have nothing at all to do with you, but a work God needs to do in the heart of another person or situation. Only God can see the entire picture, and He may be asking for your patience simply because what you desire isn't available yet. He could certainly give you a great runner-up, but then what would that say about Him? If you wait on Him, He'll never disappoint you with anything less than what is best and excellent. Remember, God did not give you a spirit of fear, but one of power, love, and a sound mind (2 Timothy 1:7). To say it again, God will not condemn you for a feeling, but He will watch to see what you do in the face of it. Bring your anxieties before God and allow Him to keep you strong in your wait and fill you with hope for what is to come.

Know that your Father has numbered the hairs on your head (Luke 12:7). The same God who used Daniel to prophesy thousands of years of empires rising and falling is the same God who is in control of your situation. Trust God knows exactly how each day must play out in order to bring all things into fulfillment. God is not afraid of your questions and He certainly understands when we ache for things. However, don't let go of the balance He desires. Continue to lean on Him in your time of need and ask Him to give light to your eyes (Psalm 13:1-6). In doing so, you'll begin to see things from the view of the spiritual realm instead of the earthly realm.

Caroline Klug

■ Therefore, since we have a great high priest who has gone through the heavens, Jesus the Son of God, let us hold firmly to the faith we profess. For we do not have a high priest who is unable to sympathize with our weaknesses, but we have one who has been tempted in every way, just as we are—yet was without sin. Let us then approach the Throne of grace with confidence, so that we may receive mercy and find grace to help us in our time of need. Hebrews 4:14-16

The Waiting Room

Remind | When, God, When?

*Humble yourselves, therefore,
under God's mighty hand, that He
may lift you up in due time.
1 Peter 5:6*

I constantly struggle with wanting things in my timing. I'm sure you can relate, and maybe even experienced some of the painful consequences of stepping out in front of God's timing. We get impatient and we try to *do* something, which is usually just us getting in the way and making our wait even longer. The amazing works of His hands come from just that – His hands. What God is asking from all of us is faith in His timing.

I am by nature, a doer. Rather than embrace the wait with joyful expectation, my initial reaction is usually to feel I have to *do* something. Immediately. Because of the way I'm wired, I've found myself in a few situations where I've stepped out in front of God and pursued a path I thought would get me there. However pure my motive was for wanting to be obedient to what God had shown me, it was still disobedience, because I was trying to make something happen in my timing rather than waiting on God's. In those situations where I drew outside the lines, the enemy had a field day. He launched his assault and I ended up dazed and confused over the attack that hit me. Then I got emotional and began asking God where I missed Him. Sound familiar? If so, I encourage you to consider the advice God placed on my own heart. Take a step back and stop pursuing what you're only being asked to *wait for* in faith.

God gives gifts as He sees fit, in order to accomplish His work (1 Corinthians 12:8-10, 27-28). Faith is one of those gifts. Everyone is asked to have faith, but it can also be a gift above and beyond believing in God as Savior. It can be a gift for faith in God as Lord of the impossible.

> **Don't pursue what you're only being asked to wait for in faith.**

The bigger the dreams God has planted in your heart, the more He's probably working on you, on a daily basis, to build a faith to endure through trials and challenges. God can do anything overnight, but big dreams usually take time to fully birth. You will encounter tests that might leave you questioning. You will see things with your earthly eyes that leave you doubting. When those things happen, you need to be quick to protect your faith in what God has spoken to you. Double down in the Word to replace doubt with confidence in who He is and excitement for what He'll do. Working on that might just be the easy part. The harder part is that annoying little question we ask way too often: "When, God, when?"

When God speaks dreams or promises into our hearts, incredible things happen inside us. We find our hearts aligning with those dreams and the passions inside of us growing in exponential proportions. Passions are a tricky thing. They are beautiful and motivating but, if left

The Waiting Room

unchecked, can cause you to step out ahead of God. Instead of being impatient and possibly even reckless, have patience and allow them to unfold in His timing. If you can bring yourself to a place of trust, you'll find yourself continually amazed and excited when He opens the door to another piece of the puzzle. Instead of feeling frustrated, you can marvel at watching it unfold like a beautiful sunset. All the things you're waiting in faith for should be accompanied by peace and patience. God is over every desire of your heart. As you walk along your spiritual path, maturing in the knowledge of God, your question of why things are not happening should naturally transform into praising the One who will bring the right things to pass in His perfect timing. Let Him use the journey you're on to build and grow your faith.

> **Passions are beautiful and motivating but, if left unchecked, can cause you to step out ahead of God.**

📖 Trust in the LORD with all your heart and lean not on your own understanding; in all your ways submit to Him, and He will make your paths straight. Proverbs 3: 5-6

Caroline Klug

Remind | Where the Air is Clear

> For since the creation of the world God's
> invisible qualities – His eternal power and
> divine nature – have been clearly seen,
> being understood from what has been
> made, so that men are without excuse.
> Romans 1:20

Simply put, the majesty of nature makes it impossible for man to contest the existence of God. We have no excuse for looking around us and still having doubt.

My husband and I live in Wisconsin. When the weather is nice, which is about five months out of the year, I like to frequent a favorite trail at High Cliff State Park. God has blessed me with many messages there, and I recall a visit there one spring when He did not disappoint. I'm convinced seeing God's messages within nature will never stop thrilling me. On this particular hike, He blessed me with an unexpected message of encouragement. Even though it was all about the hike, I knew deeply in my spirit that He was giving me insight into my trials, too. I pray the message I have to share with you today not only speaks to your heart but gives you the same encouragement it gave me.

Caroline Klug

To say I was excited to hit the trail was an understatement. I pulled up to the State Park office window, purchased my annual sticker, and parked in the front lot. I turned on my music and started on my way. In an instant, the beauty of the morning was rudely interrupted by the swarm of bugs flying around me. It only took me a second to realize what they were. For those of you who have the pleasure of living near or on a lake, you are most likely very familiar with this seasonal swarm called mayflies. For about a two-week period, these mayflies hatch and are as thick as locusts. It was an obstacle I had not anticipated. As I thought hard about turning around, God spoke His first message to my heart. "Press on. Obstacles will be there, and they may not be easy to walk through but, if you do, you will reap the rewards of having finished the race." Despite the irritation, I was determined to press on. I just hoped they wouldn't be as bad once I was deeper into the woods.

Sometimes things aren't what we hope for. The swarm continued, but so did I. Honestly, there were moments I thought I might freak out because so many of them landed on me at once, but then God shared His second message with me. He said, "If you stop now, the attack will only get worse, and it'll be that much harder and take that much longer to get out." How true of our spiritual attacks. If we give up in the middle, we're giving the enemy ground to surround us and overtake us. The message is to get up and keep walking. I know you can.

> **If we give up in the middle, we're giving the enemy ground to surround us and overtake us.**

The Waiting Room

There's an ascent in the middle of the trail that challenges me. It's very steep, and I'm always tempted to stop in the middle to rest. Through some past lessons in perseverance, God showed me the importance of pressing on and not losing my momentum, even when it gets difficult. I had a long and tough workout the night before, so my muscles were already a bit fatigued. I recalled those past messages on perseverance and began my climb. By the time I reached the top, my need for air was greater than the shallow breathing I had been doing to avoid sucking in a mayfly or ten. I didn't need the extra protein. I couldn't seem to get enough air in to keep going. I felt God very specifically urging me to keep moving no matter what.

In obedience, I kept walking, but I began praying for air. I asked God to clear the bugs long enough for me to take in enough air to recover. Within a few footsteps, the mayflies cleared completely away and I found myself taking in deep breaths as though I had been drowning and was now coming up for air. This was the third message: "When reprieve comes, even if it's only for a moment, when you find yourself where the air is clear, it's important to take in deep breaths." When your air clears of trials and obstacles, or the attacks are not as great, your strength is being replenished as you immerse yourself in God's Word and quality time with Him. This is important for when the attacks come. And they *will* come. Except this time, you'll have a deep well to draw from right from the start.

It may seem silly that God used something as simple as a mayfly to teach me a lesson, but as our beginning Scripture says, God can be clearly seen and understood by the things He made. There are so many lessons in everything around us. We just have to pray to have ears to hear and eyes to see them.

Press on even when you encounter obstacles that seem difficult. Trust that God will be with you as you put one foot in front of the other. I walked the last half mile of my hike slowly, and felt disappointed in myself for that. As I came to the end of the trail, my Father said to my heart, "It doesn't matter that you weren't running. What matters to Me is that you kept going."

> Consider it pure joy, my brothers, whenever you face trials of many kinds, because you know that the testing of your faith develops perseverance. Perseverance must finish its work so that you may be mature and complete, not lacking anything. James 1:2-3

The Waiting Room

Remind | War of Wills

> We have not stopped praying for you and asking God to fill you with the knowledge of His will through all spiritual wisdom and understanding. And we pray this in order that you may live a life worthy of the Lord and may please Him in every way: bearing fruit in every good work, growing in the knowledge of God, being strengthened with all power according to His glorious might so that you may have great endurance and patience, and joyfully giving thanks to the Father who has qualified you to share in the inheritance of the saints in the kingdom of light.
> Colossians 1:9-12

In high school, I was a debater and a mock trial attorney. I loved the challenge of presenting my cases, and the thrill of having four minutes to throw together an eight-minute award-winning speech. As much as I appreciate the ways God used that to begin equipping me for His work in speaking and teaching, I had to learn that presenting my case to God on how I thought He should do things was about as useful as the egg separator I finally donated to Goodwill.

Caroline Klug

I recall a time when I felt like a small child who wanted my way, and I put a great deal of energy into constructing lofty arguments to God on why I should get my way. I was in the process of one of these well-structured arguments when He brought me faithfully to Colossians, to the beginning Scripture. When my eyes hit the passage, I barely made it to the end through the tears welling up in my eyes. I went back and read it again, and again, and yes, again. The only word that left my lips was, "Wow." On God's instruction, I then went back and began reading it aloud, this time replacing the word "you" with "I" or "me." I believe God graced my eyes with these passages as a tender reminder of what's important. It's not about what we think is best. It's about what He knows is best.

> **It's not about what we think is best.
> It's about what He knows is best.**

It's not the arguments you present that are meaningful to God, but your heart-felt acceptance of His much bigger plan. The passage at the beginning of the chapter doesn't say you should pray to be filled with knowledge of your own situations based on your own understandings. It says you should pray to be filled with the knowledge of God's *will* through all *spiritual* wisdom and understanding. He's stretching you here to lean not on your own understanding, but to seek His will over your own individual wants and desires. We can't possibly see all that God sees. We can't possibly know what's best to pray for with the limited view we have. That's why it's so important to pray for God's will in things and ask Him to give us spiritual eyes. In the process, He'll take care of the desires of our hearts as well (Proverbs 3:5-6).

The Waiting Room

God teaches us that nothing we may want that is of this world compares to the surpassing greatness of knowing Him (Philippians 3:7-9). This doesn't mean we won't ever struggle with wanting what our flesh wants. I do think it means that, as we mature in our relationships with God, and mature in our understanding of His greater good, over time, the natural desires of our hearts will align more closely with His, and we will find peace, joy, and fulfillment in those things.

When you find yourself in doubt over whether or not it's okay to pray for something, try filtering it through Scripture. If it's there in black and white, don't justify it away. Just follow it. Not everything we walk through is neatly defined in God's Word. Life would be pretty easy if we could turn to the book of Matthew to see whether we should buy the Toyota or the Nissan. However, this is where it becomes important to know and hold to the spiritual promises of our God, seeking only His face in times of need and trusting that He'll bring the best outcome to pass. Remember, He wrote the Book. He is the Author of life. Every one of your days has been ordained before one of them has or will come to pass (Psalm 139:16). Trust that He knows what He's doing and He's never wrong – in action or in timing.

Lastly, I want to impress on you the incredible supernatural power of the Word. God tells us we battle not against flesh and blood (Ephesians 6:12). Because of that, the weapons we ought to use are not weapons of this world, but the Sword of the Spirit, which is God's Word (Ephesians 6:17). Jesus defeated Satan, when tempted, by speaking out the Word of God. This is our example. You can speak the Word out loud as a weapon against what

Caroline Klug

Satan is trying to do in your mind. Do not underestimate the power of the Word, which is living and breathing and sharper than any double-edged sword (Hebrews 4:12). Use this supernatural tool that is available to you, and you will see your mind and life changing in unimaginable ways.

    If it's a war of wills at play, pushing for your own usually produces less than desirable results. The sooner you exchange your desires for His, the sooner you'll find joy and the peace that surpasses all understanding (Philippians 4:7). We need to stop focusing so much on the things of this world that we desire and, instead, seek His beautiful face. In doing so, we'll reap a harvest of blessings, both spiritual and earthly. The Word of God is supernatural in strength and, when spoken, supernatural in power. Jesus is your Deliverer, but if you need deliverance from your situation, know what the Word says and the promises that are yours. Speak them forth and, in doing so, you'll allow the Spirit to breathe new life into both your mind and your circumstances.

◻ For the Word of God is living and active. Sharper than any double-edged sword, it penetrates even to dividing soul and spirit, joints and marrow; it judges the thoughts and attitudes of the heart. Hebrews 4:12

Remind | Walk by Faith

For we walk by faith, not by sight.
2 Corinthians 5:7

We exercise some level of faith in almost everything we do. It can be as big as looking to God for a physical healing, or as small as believing our vehicles' brakes will work properly. Every day our faith is challenged by what's going on around us and the logical reasoning happening inside us. This can be very challenging, but God calls us to lift our eyes off the things of this world and on to Him who is able to do immeasurably more than we could ever ask or imagine (Ephesians 3:20). Faith is an investment that will always produce an amazing return.

We are curious and inquisitive creatures. God placed these characteristics in us for a purpose. That ultimate purpose is to seek our Creator. However, like every other good thing God has given us, Satan perverts that natural inclination to cause confusion and separate us from God. We rally when we hear the voice of God in our hearts and minds and hold fiercely to what He has spoken to us. Opposition comes, and suddenly we're faced with the question of our loyalty, torn between the words God spoke to us and the confusion the enemy placed before us. Our beginning Scripture tells us we shouldn't react to the tangible circumstances we see with our earthly eyes. Instead, we should use our spiritual eyes to react to what God shows us in His Word or speaks to our hearts. If you're only looking around with your earthly eyes, that opposition can haunt your mind and steal your hope. It's in these times you can likely sense God's question of whether or not you will still believe no matter what you see.

There are times where God will ask you to step out and do something that might seem scary and may even produce an outcome that looks contrary to what He spoke. You'll recognize these situations because your flesh may not want to do them, but in your spirit, you know you're being asked. If God is asking you to be anywhere, there's no safer place to be. No matter how frightening it seems, or how uncertain the response it produces, if you walk where God tells you, His protection will be with you. I can tell you from experience it can be a painful, and even humiliating, road at times to stand in faith over the things unseen. However, you'll never see your promise manifest without first stepping out in faith. It wouldn't be faith if you waited to see it and *then* stepped out.

> **It wouldn't be faith if you waited to see it and *then* stepped out.**

One of the biggest enemies to our faith is our need for reasoning. Things happen around us, and we try to figure out what they mean. We try to figure out if God is for our dream or against it. When emotions are engaged, this becomes an even more complicated process, especially if answers are not readily available. This will naturally lead people to making assumptions, which the enemy has a field day with. All Satan sees is an opportunity to play with your emotions and break your heart. Satan will take whatever you are seeing and figure out a way to twist it so it looks like opposition. He'll use it to break your hope and get you to stop believing in your dream or promise altogether. I may be talking about your promise, but please know the enemy's role goes much deeper than that. I like the way Pastor Adam Jackson said it, "Satan's active role is to oppose God. He desires for us to doubt, distrust and disobey God. Satan is against us because he is against God. God is for us (Romans 8:31). Our aim should be to trust [God] despite the difficulties we face or the lies of the enemy."

Emotion, and the reasoning that accompanies it, are very powerful forces that require great discipline on our behalf. If we don't learn to bring them captive before Christ and rely on Him to reveal the truth, we're destined for a train wreck.

Through our journeys, we battle our selfish ambitions and desires. We watch God transform our hearts to hold the desires that are pleasing to Him. We learn our lessons of humility as we see the hand of God move in ways we never imagined. In the end, we realize that where God brought us has fulfilled our desires more than anything we could have hoped for. Every ounce of the struggle was worth what it did for our faith, and our increased ability to endure through Christ who strengthens us (1 Peter 4:11). Oswald Chambers said it beautifully: "Are we prepared for God to stamp out our personal ambitions? Are we prepared for God to destroy our individual decisions by supernaturally transforming them? It will mean not knowing why God is taking us that

Caroline Klug

way, because knowing would make us spiritually proud. We never realize at the time what God is putting us through – we go through it more or less without understanding. Then suddenly we come to a place of enlightenment and realize – 'God has strengthened me and I didn't even know it!'"

> Now to Him who is able to do immeasurably more than all we ask or imagine, according to His power that is at work within us, to Him be glory in the church and in Christ Jesus throughout all generations, for ever and ever! Amen. Ephesians 3:20-21

Remind | The Peace of God

> Do not be anxious about anything, but in everything, by prayer and petition, with thanksgiving, present your requests to God. And the peace of God, which transcends all understanding, will guard your hearts and your minds in Christ Jesus.
> Philippians 4:6-7

This is such a powerful verse. God is making a promise to you. If you give Him all the things that cause you worry and uncertainty, He will replace those feelings with a peace you can't explain. In order to realize this amazing display of His power, you'll need to follow the instructions He's giving in the verses right before it. Once you do, you can act in confidence and rest in the peace that follows. Let's take a look at what He's teaching us to do.

God instructs us to present our requests by prayer and petition. The Greek word for petition is *aitema*, coming from *aiteo*, which means, to ask, beg, call for, crave, desire, or require. These words paint a wonderful picture of reverent desperation. He's giving us insight into what our prayer time with Him should look like. If you're struggling with something, don't just say a ten-second prayer and call it a day. Steal away to a quiet place, get on your knees, and cry out to Him. Share your heart. Pray the Scriptures. Make the time, then take the time. God sees the investment and it won't return void. Time spent in prayer is an investment that will strengthen your relationship with God, when done with a heart that longs to hear His voice.

The second part of our instruction tells us to present our petitions with thanksgiving. Interestingly, the Greek word for thanksgiving is defined as an act of worship. The word *eucharistia* actually comes from two Greek words; the first word *"eu"* meaning good, and the second, *"charis"* meaning divine influence upon, and its reflection in the life. How do we come before God with a heart of worship, knowing He is able? How do we come before God, willing to give to Him divine influence over our situation, ready to obey whatever He tells us? Relationship, that's how. When you make Christ the inward treasure of your soul, He becomes an outward reflection in your life. The more you know about who He is, the more you'll naturally want to praise Him. The deeper you get into His Word, the more reason you'll have to praise Him.

> **When you make Christ the inward treasure of your soul, He becomes an outward reflection in your life.**

There's another element we don't want to miss. The praise isn't just because of who He is, but it's also an act of faith in declaring the works He *will* do in and over your life. There are several examples in Scripture where people, including Jesus, gave praise to God *before* the miracle they asked for occurred. It was the exclamation

The Waiting Room

point on their statement of faith. Moses praised God before He parted the Red Sea (Exodus 14:13). Jesus praised God before He raised Lazarus from the dead (John 11: 41-42).

Here's the most exciting part. When we can come to God in worship with our request, and with a heart that resolves to love Him and obey His response, our crown is a peace that transcends the deepest area of our understanding. It's a peace that rises above and overcomes the initial emotions that brought us before God in the first place. This is completely supernatural and only producible by the Holy Spirit at work within us. Peace doesn't always remove grief, pain, or the issue at hand. Instead, it rises above those emotions or situations to create a restful spirit in you – one who believes God is at work for the good of those who love Him (Romans 8:28). God will use that peace to guard your heart and mind in Christ Jesus – again and again. God knows Satan lives to attack and bring doubt on what He speaks to you. When you receive peace over a situation and Satan attempts to place doubt in your mind to rob you of that peace, God will use His Holy Spirit to recall in you the peace He once spoke over you. It's a gentle and sweet reminder, and a powerful weapon against attack that you can claim in any moment of any day.

What a beautiful love God has for us, to provide us with such an amazing gift. Peace is a powerful tool in helping to determine if we're on God's path. Once you make your request known to God, allow it to remain at His feet. In return, He'll bless you with an assurance that creates rest deep within you. Whether immediately or in time, guidance will come, but always keep your eye on

Caroline Klug

Jesus, and peace will follow. May the peace of God guard your heart and mind in Christ Jesus.

> ◼ And we know that in all things God works for the good of those who love Him, who have been called according to His purpose.... For I am convinced that neither death nor life, neither angels nor demons, neither the present nor the future, nor any powers, neither height nor depth, nor anything else in all creation, will be able to separate us from the love of God that is in Christ Jesus our Lord. Romans 8:28, 38

Remind | Milk and Honey

> The Lord said, "I have indeed seen the misery of my people in Egypt. I have heard them crying out because of their slave drivers, and I am concerned about their suffering. So I have come down to rescue them from the hand of the Egyptians and to bring them up out of that land into a good and spacious land, a land flowing with milk and honey."
> Exodus 3:7-8

In spite of your best intentions, you might find yourself in a place of doubt while you wait. You may feel God is being silent in your circumstances and wonder if He hears your cry for help. You don't see your circumstance changing and, because of that, allow time to be an enemy to your faith. Please know the eyes and ears of God never fail Him. He sees all, He hears all, and He knows all. You only need to trust that when His timing is right, He'll come with the fire of His Spirit and light a way through the darkest of circumstances.

Remember that burning bush? In the beginning Scripture, God is speaking to Moses on Mt. Horeb. He's telling Moses that He has seen the oppression of His people and has come to deliver them out of a land of distress and into one of delight. When I read that, I imagine God using the word "indeed" as an answer to the secret question in Moses' heart. The Israelites waited to be delivered from under the rule of the Egyptian pharaohs for four hundred years. The sheer number of their collective prayers and tears would be enough to fill the deepest of oceans. Moses must have wondered where his God was, and if He was seeing this great oppression. God's response to Moses is, "Indeed I have seen." One of my favorite verses, Matthew 10:30, reminds us that the very hairs on our heads are numbered. That speaks of a God who knows infinitely more than we could ever imagine. He hears you.

> **God hears you.**

In Psalm 139:3-4, the Word tells us God discerns every move we make. To discern something is to recognize or identify it before it comes into our plain sight. This Scripture tells us He is familiar with every one of our ways and knows every thought on our mind before we even attempt to speak. You might have a lot of thoughts and ideas about something whirling around in your mind, but God knows them more completely than you ever could. He knows how you operate. He knows how you think about things and the tendencies you have to react in certain ways and why. He created you. He knit you together in your mother's womb and is intimately aware of everything that makes you tick (Psalm 139:13). He is more than aware of every desire, hurt, question, longing, dream, and thought you have.

Just as doubt has a brother called fear, so our mind has a similar brother. A friend once said to me that our mind is an enemy of God. Its brother? Time. Most of us

The Waiting Room

struggle with impatience. We think God's deliverance from our circumstances should be as easy as the drive-thru windows that litter our nation. We place our orders and expect God to hand us a Happy Meal. Fortunately for us, we'll never hear God ask if we'd like fries with that train wreck. There are times when God does move quickly but, often, He takes His time for a reason. God never does anything without purpose. He is love (1 John 4:8) and, for that reason, you can believe God won't make you wait in something that causes you pain unless He knows it's ultimately for your benefit. There may be something He needs to grow within you, or a blessing He knows is yet to come that just takes a little time to birth.

God not only hears you, but is deeply moved by you. We lack complete knowledge and understanding, making us weak in our flesh. That knowledge and understanding is one of the things God is made of and makes Him strong and infallible. Trust that He knows what you don't. Give it to Him, and then trust He'll return to you what is best. He loves you passionately and doesn't want to see you in a land of waste. He wants to see you in a land flowing with milk and honey. The Israelites had forty years to wander and wonder. Despite all the miracles, they struggled with doubt on more than one occasion. God didn't fail them. Rather, in His perfect timing, He came with the fire of His Spirit and lit a way through the darkest of their circumstances, bringing them home to the Promised Land (Joshua 1). He won't fail you, either. If you wait expectantly for Him, I promise you will not be disappointed.

Caroline Klug

❏ "For I am the Lord, your God, who takes hold of your right hand and says to you, Do not fear; I will help you. Do not be afraid, O worm Jacob, O little Israel, for I Myself will help you," declares the Lord, your Redeemer, the Holy One of Israel. Isaiah 41:13-14

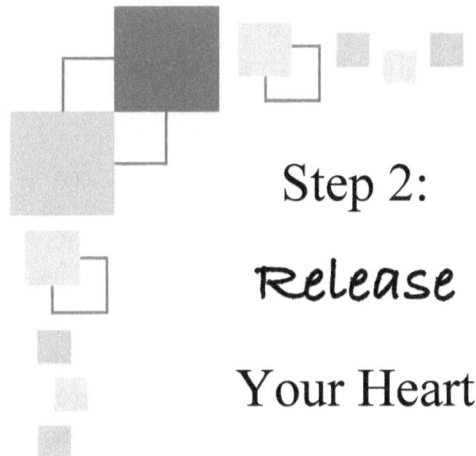

Step 2:
Release
Your Heart

Now that we've reminded our hearts of who God is and how He's working, we can draw a deep breath of spiritual peace into our lungs and breathe out all that anxiety. Are you feeling a little better? I hope so. Allowing God to take you through it in order to get to it requires all the things we've talked about so far, but this next step is crucial.

I won't lie to you. This is the most difficult step. Releasing your heart – your desires, needs, fears, and expectations – can be incredibly difficult. But it's also incredibly rewarding. It will change you for the better from the "heart-side" out. It will make you stronger and wiser. It will be the difference between dwelling in hurt and being joyful with expectancy. It might even be the difference between entering your promised land or continuing to wander in the desert for another long and dry season.

Even though you're on your knees, you might, intentionally or unintentionally, be keeping your need in your lap instead of lifting it as an offering to God. This is where the rubber meets the road. This is where you make a life altering decision on who you trust more – yourself or God. Before we tackle the big "T" word, let's look at a few reasons we might struggle to let go and give the situations we face over to God.

We Want the Wrong Things

The first one is simple. We want the wrong things. As human beings, we were born with a sinful nature. It's innate in us to want to be selfish. Take a toddler, for example: if they find a candy bar on the table, do you think that small child is thinking about giving it back to you because they really shouldn't be eating it? My guess is no. To them, it looks great and might be just what they think they need. Most children would grab and run. In fact, the only thing they might be thinking is how far they need to go to get away from you so they can eat the entire candy bar before you're able to stop them. That visual gives me an appreciation for what God must feel when He sees us grabbing for something we shouldn't. What is it my teenage daughter used to say? Facepalm.

When you desire the things of this world over the things of God, you'll find little fulfillment. The things of this world may seem satisfying in the moment but will leave you feeling empty and on the continual hunt for more. It will make your wait feel even longer and that much harder. If you find yourself in this situation, go to God and confess it, and allow Him to reshape what's really at the core of your worry into something within His will for your life.

The Waiting Room

Emotions

Another thing that can get in the way of giving things over to God is our emotions. We don't have time to go through all of them, but I think an honorable mention goes out to those useless yet controlling emotions like anger, unforgiveness and doubt. These are messy feelings, because they blind us to the reality God operates in. Every one of these emotions is a result of a lack of knowledge or trust in who God is (there's that "T" word again). They skew our perspective and cause us to operate within our field of vision rather than God's. When we operate outside of God's field of vision, we're likely to miss doors He has hanging wide open for us. We'll be too busy focusing on the toe we just stubbed and walk right past it. This results in yet another lap around the desert.

Manna, anyone?

Running the Play

Speaking of manna, let's talk about times we run ahead of God into the Promised Land. You know what I mean – that God-given promise or dream you have burning inside you. Even this is subject to letting go. Let me explain. One of the most well-intentioned, yet misguided reasons for hanging onto something so tightly, is because we *know* God spoke it to or over us. Whether it's the promise of physical healing, a new job, a repaired marriage, a new ministry or having a baby, all of these things are subject to God's plan and His timing. If you're anything like me, you like to try to figure God out. You try to get three steps ahead of Him and figure out *how* He's going to accomplish something. Then you run the play because, hey, you're just trying to be a good teammate and help a guy out, right?

Wrong. I can promise you (from a lot of personal experience) this is one of the fastest ways to foul things up and delay your blessing. Even if what you're waiting for is God-given, it's always a good idea to give it back to God and let Him fulfill it when and how He sees fit. Sometimes He'll require action of you. In those times He'll make that clear if you're listening. Other times, He'll ask you to simply rest and let Him work behind the scenes. You type A personalities (like me) don't always have to be doing something.

Hanging on to What's Wrong

The last one we're going to talk about is by no means least. It's a powerful one – powerful and very destructive. A lot of life experiences led to someone coining the phrase, "Hindsight is 20/20." When I reflect back through the seasons in my life, the reasons for spending so much time wandering aimlessly through the wilderness are crystal clear to me. But some of the most profound times of my being in the valley of darkness was because of fear. I was waiting on God to meet a desire of my heart, but I wasn't sure what was ahead of me, so I was afraid to let go of what I already had. Even if it was ugly and barren, I still hung on with both hands and maybe a few toes. It was all I knew, and fear whispered lies that if I let go of it, I would end up with nothing or something worse. What is it they say? Better the devil you know than the devil you don't. If you follow the bread crumbs, you're likely

The Waiting Room

to find there is one most logical root cause for hanging on to what's wrong, while you wait for what's right. Let's be honest with each other. It's a backup. It's our Plan B in case God doesn't come through. Ouch. That kind of hurt to write. This brings us full circle to the big "T" word we started with. Let's rip the Band-Aid off and get to it.

Raising the Wall

Trust can be a painful word for some people. Unfortunate or even traumatic situations in life can create trust issues that go outside the bounds of reason. Raising the wall becomes a learned defense mechanism to avoid hurt. I'm sure you've heard this before, but people will always disappoint you. People are imperfect, and even the best-intentioned individual can mess up. We make a huge mistake by putting God in the same category as people. When we're guessing what God might do based on our past experiences with people, we're not comparing apples to apples. That's more like comparing apples to orangutans.

You might be wondering if you can trust God enough to completely let go of the situation you're facing. I know the wait is hard, and the unknown is even harder. What isn't unknown is God's character. God is the same yesterday, today, and forever (Hebrews 13:8). God is love (1 John 4:7-8). I love what the Amplified version of the Bible says for 1 Corinthians 1:9:

"God is faithful [He is reliable, trustworthy and ever true to His promise—He can be depended on], and through Him you were called into fellowship with His Son, Jesus Christ our Lord."

When we started this book, the first step we went through was all about reminding our hearts who God is and how He operates. We learned He's someone we can rely on and trust in. I hope what you've read so far has helped your heart to be open to this next step, trusting Him with what He decides is best to give back to you.

An Important Disclaimer

Before you jump excitedly into letting go (I'm trying to make that sound less scary), I need to clarify what I'm *not* talking about. When I say let go, that doesn't mean give up. Don't give up on a marriage that feels dead. Don't give up on a loved one who doesn't know Jesus. Don't give up on a God-given dream that looks impossible. Marriage, salvation and fulfilling God's calling on your life are all within God's good and perfect will, along with so many others I could never have time to list out. I'm not asking you to give up. I'm asking you to *let go* and *let God*.

Let's keep going.

Release | Letting Go

> "For I am the Lord, your God, who takes hold
> of your right hand and says to you, Do not
> fear; I will help you. Do not be afraid, O worm
> Jacob, O little Israel, for I Myself will help
> you," declares the Lord, your Redeemer,
> the Holy One of Israel.
> Isaiah 41:13-14

There's a story you might have heard about a mountain climber. The story tells of a man whose aim was to climb the highest of mountains. He was full of pride and longed for the glory of accomplishing such an incredible feat, so he set out to climb the vast mountain range all alone. The darkness of night fell over the landscape, and the moon and stars were covered by clouds. He could no longer see anything. In spite of having no visibility, he continued on. He was only a few feet from the top when he lost his balance and began the terrifying fall downward. In his petrified state, he shut his eyes and imagined how close death was. He was shocked to suddenly feel the rope tighten around his waist and snap him back. There he remained, suspended by the rope, with nothing but blackness around him. In that moment he had no choice but to cry out, "Help me, God!"

Caroline Klug

God asked the man if he believed He could save him, to which the man replied, "Of course."

After a moment of silence, the man heard God speak gently. "If you believe in who I am, cut the rope."

Once again, terror seized him and he gripped the rope with more fervor than before. He was too scared and wouldn't trust. The next morning, a rescue team found him suspended from the rope, dead and frozen, hands still gripping the rope. He was hanging only a few feet from a wide, flat ledge.

This story is fictitious in nature, but its reality is played out many times over in each of our lives. We're faced with situations that force us to exercise what we really believe. The ropes in our lives represent the things we choose to be dependent on rather than God. We allow ourselves to believe people, habits, or material items can bring us a sense of security or well-being. It's kind of ironic, given these are usually the things that produce the insecurity we feel, leading to emotional and spiritual sickness. Our patriarchal fathers, like Abraham, Isaac, and Jacob, understood how these ropes can entrap us. Each of these leaders faced a series of struggles until they eventually achieved the character necessary to cut their ropes and rely solely on God. The same God who set their courses from the beginning of time is the same God we serve today. He's the only One capable of taking hold of your right hand and rescuing you.

In the Scripture at the beginning of this chapter, God is talking to Jacob and encouraging him to have hope. I find it interesting that God tells Jacob, not once, but twice, not to be afraid. Although these are different words in the New International Version (fear, afraid),

The Waiting Room

they have the same Hebrew root. God doesn't strike me as someone who needs to repeat Himself. We can't know this for sure, but let's entertain a possible explanation.

Commentaries suggest the use of the term "worm" for Jacob denotes his frailty and detested condition in exile, forced to crawl, possibly even into the earth, for safety. This paints a good picture of the physical, mental, and emotional condition. Fear can be powerful. It's defined as an emotion we experience in anticipation of some specific pain or danger. It's usually accompanied by a desire to fight or flee. God told him not to fear to ease his mind. As with all good humans, I'm guessing the comfort of those words lasted about as long as a chocolate bar would in my house. Although we can't read Jacob's mind, my guess is that as quickly as he felt comfort, fear crept back in and his mind went immediately back to the questions of when or how. Sound familiar? I have to wonder if that's why God says it again. To really get Jacob's attention and let His words sink in. If God's telling you not to be afraid, you can trust that it's because He's got this in His very capable hands. He has a plan.

You might be facing a faith walk that's requiring every ounce of everything you have. Maybe you've come to a point where you're tired, afraid, doubtful, and even hopeless.

> **God has a plan.**

Maybe you think you can't take another step. If you let Him, your Redeemer can step in and encourage you in who He is, and help you not to abandon the good fight. He'll remind you of the victory waiting around the corner. If you're human, this probably produces mixed emotions. On one hand, you're comforted. On the other, you recognize that God is asking you to get up and keep walking into the thing that's been sucking the life out of you. You might feel like you can't do it.

Let me close by pointing out some of the sweetest words of this Scripture. Lean in a little, because they are really good:

"'I Myself will help you,' declares the Lord."

I underline a lot of things in my Bible, but I rarely write words in it. But next to this sentence, I wrote, "This is very personal." We serve a personal God. That's one of the many things which sets Him apart. The promises of our patriarchal fathers are our promises as well, and God is hammering a very personal stake in the ground to assure you of His help. We've been that dejected soul who feels terrified and left without hope. Don't fall victim to your circumstances and grasp more tightly on to the rope that will eventually hang you. Instead, cry out to the One who can save you, and then walk in the direction He gives you with faith and trust. God sends help in a lot of different forms, but His specificity of saying "I Myself" brings a whole new meaning to the mix. Cut the rope. As you take that step of faith through obedience, He will take hold of your right hand and you will not fall (Psalm 37:24).

◼ Though he stumble, he will not fall, for the Lord upholds him with His hand.
Psalm 37:24

The Waiting Room

Release | A New Thing (Part 1)

> Forget the former things; do not dwell on
> the past. See, I am doing a new thing!
> Now it springs up; do you not perceive it?
> I am making a way in the desert
> and streams in the wasteland.
> Isaiah 43:18-19

Can you imagine a wasteland? Merriam-Webster defines this as "an ugly, often devastated or barely inhabitable place or area." Barely inhabitable. Even writing those words sends a quietness through me, as I humbly remember a time when I felt like the world was passing me by. My hopes, my dreams, my ambitions. They all seemed to be getting in the car and driving into the big city while I remained tied up in this suburb named Disappointment. I felt strongly that God had more for my life, but I couldn't seem to get past what my earthly eyes saw. Rather than see my present circumstances as a waiting room, I saw them as a destination. Maybe even a punishment.

Punishment. Yes, I went there. Admit it, you've had the thought a time or two. God won't answer my prayers because I didn't do what He told me. Or, more transparently, God won't because I did something I shouldn't have. I wrote the book on this one. Well, I hope to someday. For now, let's just say I've made my share of mistakes. I had God-sized dreams burning in me, but I let Satan use my past to hold me down for a long time. I let him tell me a woman who had been divorced twice couldn't possibly be used the way God was speaking to my heart. I tortured myself with the notion of unfulfilled dreams. Letting those lies in limited my ability to believe and my desire to step out in faith. It kept me tied up and feeling sorry for myself, rather than on my knees in prayer with fervent expectation.

We can all feel tied up for different reasons. If there's something sinful in your life, there's an obvious answer. I didn't say it would be easy, just obvious. You need to repent and stop whatever sin is getting in between you and the promises of God. Sin is a cancer and it needs to be cut out. Surgically and swiftly. No looking back. It's the only way to be free of it and its negative effects. The longer you leave it there, the sicker you'll get until it eventually kills you. If you've been brave enough to walk through repentance, and it's the shame of past sin holding you down, then you need to allow God to cover you with forgiveness. It's nothing more than lies if you think God won't bless you or answer your prayers because of past sin. If you've repented and asked for forgiveness, then your sin is as far from you as the east is from the west (Psalm 103:12). Holding onto that is holding onto the very thing God may want to use to help others.

What about those unfulfilled dreams? Maybe you have something, even God-given, burning in your heart, and not seeing the manifestation of it is causing you to lose hope. If that's the case, I'm happy to say the answer

The Waiting Room

is much easier. You simply need to change your glasses. You need to make a decision to see things through His eyes rather than yours. Remember when we talked about moving mountains? Remember the supernatural power available to you through the Holy Spirit? This is where things get really exciting.

Think once more about that barely inhabitable place. Now imagine what would happen if a stream of fresh, clean water is planted right in the middle of that wasteland. Very slowly, over time, the ground around it will begin to absorb that water. As the water spreads farther into the ground, it's the catalyst for new life. Slowly, those seeds that once fell on hard and dry soil now have soft dirt to cultivate in. In a matter of time, what was once ugly and barren is full of lush, green life. As amazing as this process is, it does require time and patience. If you're praying for change and see no immediate effects, don't be discouraged. Instead, think about what God is saying about making streams in the wasteland. When you choose to call God the Lord of your life, you're choosing life itself. You're allowing His living water to be deposited into the deepest part of you (John 7:38). You're allowing God to put that stream right into the very heart of your being, to revive, refresh, and renew. You only have to drink from it and let that Holy Spirit power pour over every part of you.

> **In a matter of time, what was once ugly and barren is full of lush, green life.**

That repository of water is very satisfying to your soul, but that's not all it is. We return to a common scientific principle – water was meant to flow. As you read His Word and spend time with Him, increasing your understanding of who God is and His will for you, that stream of water begins to flow not only into every part of you, but into the lives of those around you. That water changes us. It changes our hearts and transforms our minds (Romans 12:2). God says people will know His children by the fruits they produce (Matthew 7:16-17). After you've taken in that living water, you'll begin to see fruit. What was once ugly and uninhabitable inside you is replaced by what is beautiful and full of life.

Don't be so quick to feel disappointed if you're still in the waiting room. God could very well be using this time to create a new stream of water inside you. That stream will not only contribute to your own promises becoming real, but will impact the hearts and lives of those around you.

> Whoever believes in me, as Scripture has said, rivers of living water will flow from within them. John 7:38

Release | A New Thing (Part 2)

> Forget the former things; do not dwell on
> the past. See, I am doing a new thing!
> Now it springs up; do you not perceive it?
> I am making a way in the desert
> and streams in the wasteland.
> Isaiah 43:18-19

In Part 1, we looked at this verse in Isaiah and discussed the effects of depositing God's living water in us, and how that pours out to the lives of those around us. I believe this Scripture also tells us something about the specific faith walks we're all journeying today, as well as offering us insight into the personality of our God.

Everyone has a filter through which they see the world. Your filter is made up of everything you choose to see and believe about yourself and the people and situations around you. When assessing the potential outcomes, you might find yourself piecing together all the points of logic that make up said filter. I was taught at an early age to always assess situations and try to understand all possible outcomes prior to making a decision. This might seem sound in reason, but it fails to be sound in spirit. God tells us in His Word not to get so bent out of shape on what we see happening from day to day, and to fix our eyes on what He's doing behind the scenes (2 Corinthians 4:18). Clearly, that was my paraphrase, but I think it holds water. We certainly need to pay attention to the things right in front of our face, but we shouldn't place so much stock in them that it overrides what God is trying to show us and tell us in our spirit. If you can truly grasp this teaching and put it into practice, I firmly believe you'll find victory in your trials. It won't make them all go away, but you'll be able to see beyond your current circumstance and rest your hope on the promise in front of you.

Look at the verse in Isaiah again. I urge you to stop and read this Scripture out loud. Can you feel the gentle push God is giving you to look to Him in spirit? Can you sense the excitement God longs to pass on to you about the amazing and life-breathing things He has for you? I can't help but picture Him, eyes shining with excitement, hands gesturing (I had to inherit this from someone), begging you to look past the preconceived notions, past wounds and common-sense deductions about what you think *should* make sense, and perceive what He's doing in the spiritual realm. *W.E. Vine's Concise Dictionary of the Bible* defines the word perceive as "gaining a full knowledge of" or "becoming fully acquainted with." In asking the question in this Scripture, He's longing for you to put aside your earthly eyes and allow Him to show you what He has for you. He wants to show you what's coming. This can't be dictated by the circumstances around us. In fact, I believe God often

The Waiting Room

allows the circumstances around us to contradict what He's spoken to us in spirit as a way to test our faith. Will we follow Him despite what we see in front of us? Will we continue to stand when the valley is filled with the stench of defeat? The ultimate show of our Christian maturity is when we can stand firmly, not only in faith, but also in joy, knowing that God will bring about His promises in due time (1 Peter 5:6, Psalm 145:15).

We serve an amazing God. Open your heart and mind and allow God to show you what only He can do through the power of His Holy Spirit living in you. Once He's given you the vision of His great glory, praise Him, put on your armor, and stand (Ephesians 6:13).

> Your kingdom is an everlasting kingdom, and Your dominion endures through all generations. The LORD is trustworthy in all He promises and faithful in all He does. The LORD upholds all who fall and lifts up all who are bowed down. The eyes of all look to You, and You give them their food at the proper time. Psalm 145: 13-15

Caroline Klug

The Waiting Room

Release | Lift Up Your Eyes

> The Lord said to Abram after Lot had parted from him, "Lift up your eyes from where you are and look north and south, east and west. All the land that you see I will give to you and your offspring forever. I will make your offspring like the dust of the earth, so that if anyone could count the dust, then your offspring could be counted."
> Genesis 13:14-16

Can you see the sparkle in your Father's eyes as He muses over the dust of the earth that He knows can't be counted by anyone other than Himself? He has an abundance of blessings just waiting to pour over you. There are so many of them that, just like Abram's offspring, they can't be counted. You may be asking yourself how you get to that place of blessing. I pray that God will give me the words to encourage your heart and enlighten you with a simple truth – you need only to lift up your eyes.

In Genesis 13:1-11, we learn Abram and his nephew Lot had grown wealthy in possession and livestock. The land they lived on couldn't support both of them and, after a while, they started to fight about it.

Caroline Klug

Abram recognized this wasn't the brotherly way to live, and suggested they part company, giving Lot his choice of land. Hold on a second. What do you think was going through Abram's mind? He had to be concerned for his own family and livestock. He also had to see what Lot saw – the well-watered plains of the Jordan on one half of the land. What caused him to selflessly step aside and allow Lot first pick? In Chapter 12, God had already spoken to Abram and promised to make him into a great nation. Out of sheer human nature, I wonder if a question may have run around in Abram's mind, causing him to wonder what might become of this "great nation" God promised if he didn't have the right kind of land to support it. I believe the same Spirit that quickened Abram to avoid strife was also the same Spirit who reminded him of the character of his God, which brought faith to his heart in this life-changing moment. Yes, Lot did choose what appeared to be the better land. However, what Abram gave up in land, he would soon find was a small investment compared to his return. It was then God reaffirmed His covenant and gave Abram eyes to see his inheritance and the faith to walk toward it, which you might recognize as The Promised Land.

Here's the really exciting part. Too often we find ourselves wounded by traps set by the enemy. We lose focus and cast our eyes downward on the pits we fall into. It consumes us and becomes the only thing we see. Our emotions only complicate what little focus we have left, and we surrender to the pain and the lies the enemy uses to convince us we have no better lot in life. I believe God is using this Scripture to send a strong answer to how you get out of the pit. God is telling you to lift up your eyes!

The Waiting Room

This is not just the retelling of an old story. This is a very specific instruction that you can still use today. He wants so badly for you to see all He has for you. Make no mistake – God has a plan for your life (Jeremiah 29:11). If you don't look beyond your circumstances, then you'll never see the inheritance He has for you, your children, and your children's children.

There's one more call to action. Once you're brave enough to look on that inheritance, you'll need to walk it out. You'll never take hold of it unless you walk the path He's asking.

> **If you don't look beyond your circumstances, you'll never see the inheritance God has for you.**

Walk it in faith. Walk it in trust. Walk it knowing beyond a shadow of a doubt that He who began a good work is faithful to complete it (Philippians 1:6).

Revelation. That's what I pray this insight gives you. A revelation that transforms your mind and renews your hope. Lift your eyes from your circumstances and look onto the future God has laid out for you. Search for it. Seek it as a precious treasure and then walk it in faith. You serve a covenant God. The covenant He made with Abram so long ago was for all of his descendants to come – including you. Embrace the blessings that are yours in Christ Jesus. Like Abram, will you dare to be a visionary for God?

Go, walk through the length and breadth of the land, for I am giving it to you.
Genesis 13:17

Caroline Klug

Release | Spring of Life (Part 1)

> ...but whoever drinks the water I give him
> will never thirst. Indeed, the water I
> give him will become in him a spring of
> water welling up to eternal life.
> John 4:14

Our God is a heart God. He's not overly concerned with what goes on around us. He's more concerned about what goes on inside us. It's in the depths of mystery that life is formed, and it's from those depths that life is poured out to those around us. For this reason, we must be very careful about what we let in. It becomes the source of what flows from us – a choice that impacts who we become and what we eventually help others to become.

Before my husband and I opted for condo life, we used to have a large yard and several gardens to take care of. Every spring, we'd need to spend a good portion of time clearing out dead plants and leaves from the flower gardens, weeding, tilling the soil in the vegetable gardens, trimming back rose bushes and, of course, the celebratory first lawn mowing of the year. One spring, as I sat pulling weeds and making room for new life, I found myself touched by the analogy. I began praying and asking God to show me what "dead" things He wanted to pull from me to make room for new things that are filled with His life. As I reflected on this prayer, I realized that planting something new does nothing unless it has a source of fresh water. Many times in life, we allow God in long enough to plant something beautiful, only to neglect watering it. Without water, it withers and dies.

Water is an essential part of all living matter. As humans, we are almost two-thirds water. When we're deprived of it, we die in a matter of days. In researching, I found water to be one of the most studied materials on earth. Despite this, it's also one of the most poorly understood in terms of behavior and function. I found myself smiling at this, as I've come to see that our God is a God of mystery. It would be just like Him to refer to Himself as living water (Jeremiah 2:13) – a material that in our fleshly wisdom, we find remarkable and mysterious all at once. In making this reference, God is simply showing us we can't have life apart from Him, and no matter how hard we look, there are no substitutes. When we ask God into our hearts as our Lord and Savior, we're allowing Him in as our source. From Him flows a stream of living water (John 7:38) that feeds our every need. It sustains health – spirit, soul, and body.

I would be remiss if I didn't mention one of the most beautiful things about this living water. As it wells within us and grows us into the vision of beauty God created, it naturally begins to flow out from us. As it does, it seeps and soaks into everything around us, penetrating the very hearts and souls of the people we're in contact with. The more we choose to drink from the water, the more growth there is.

The Waiting Room

Spring is a time of change. Allow God to deposit His spring rain into your spirit. Day by day, I'm still learning about the grace and power of this living water, but I've resolved in my heart to seek to intimately know its source (1 Corinthians 2:2). Allow Him to prune and cut back what doesn't glorify Him, and to grow only those things that do. Don't let fear keep you from embracing the new things God has waiting for you. Are you feeling void of anything but rock and dust? Are you dying of spiritual thirst? Just as He did with the woman at the well (John 4), Christ is pursuing you and offering you a drink of His living water – the water that will satisfy and quench the deepest of your desires.

> Spring is a time of change. Allow God to deposit His spring rain into your spirit.

He said to me: "It is done. I am the Alpha and the Omega, the Beginning and the End. To him who is thirsty I will give to drink without cost from the spring of the water of life. He who overcomes will inherit all this, and I will be his God and he will be My son."
Revelation 21:6-7

Caroline Klug

Release | Spring of Life (Part 2)

> ...but whoever drinks the water I give him
> will never thirst. Indeed, the water I
> give him will become in him a spring of
> water welling up to eternal life.
> John 4:14

In Part 1, we talked about the annual spring clearing of gardens and the beautiful analogy of the "dead" things God wants to pull from us to make room for new life. We serve a God who hears our prayers, and He will always be faithful to meet with us when we're seeking His will. Several years ago, I had asked God what dead things He wanted to remove from my own life to make way for the new. Although God had a divine appointment waiting for me within 24 hours of asking that question, it was preceded by a journey of years.

That next day, I was driving to church, caught by the words of a song that reminded me of my struggle with an old emotional wound of rejection. To my confusion, these emotions had been stirring and rising to the surface over many different areas over the prior few months. I was feeling inadequate about my abilities for ministry. After speaking to a group only a few days earlier, I walked away feeling like a failure and wondering if that was really my calling. As I listened to the words of that song playing in my car, I suddenly knew what He was saying and that it was time. While still driving, wishing they made windshield wipers for eyes, I cried out to God. I knew oppression was not from Him, and anything I did for His Kingdom had nothing to do with my abilities – only His. I began to praise Him and the prayer that fell from my lips surprised even me. I asked God for incredible things and they came out of my mouth before I even realized what I was asking for.

    I enjoyed worship that morning in church. I knew healing was coming and I told God I was ready. At the end of the message, there was a call for anyone who was suffering from a spiritual, emotional, or physical ailment to come to the front to meet with a prayer team. Before the pastor even made the call, I knew I was being asked. As excited as I was over the thought of healing, I found myself wrestling with that ugly thing called pride. Despite feeling a little embarrassed, I walked up there and stood awkwardly by myself. This was my home church filled with people I loved and felt comfortable with, but for some reason, I was afraid. Emotion welled up within me, but I resolved to hold it in. Eventually, a woman made her way to me and took my hands. She is with the Lord today, but at the time was a senior in our church and a strong prayer warrior. Her heart and spirit were as filled with passion for Christ as I have ever seen. After only a few moments praying, she took my face in her hands and began to pray that the spirit of rejection be gone. In that instant, I felt (other than the utter amazement of her saying that) broken and humbled and began to cry. She then began to pray the things over me I had asked God for

The Waiting Room

in my car that morning and I honestly thought my knees were going to buckle. I felt as though her frail hands were the only things keeping me standing. I opened my eyes and she was still holding my face in her hands, looking at me with eyes that could have been my Jesus. She said, "Daughter, you have asked and He will give it to you." I still tremble as I write this. I gave her a very long hug and walked slowly back to my seat. The oppression was gone. Although my head was still struggling to grasp her prayers, my spirit was released and stirred.

I don't find it surprising that over the next several months I encountered situations that tested me – things that might have previously stirred those feelings of rejection. It's not uncommon for the enemy to try to reopen a wound. It's one thing to accept the healing, but you have to remember to keep walking in it. If God has given you truth in something, hold fast to it. Through His infinite mercy and grace, you can thank God for receiving that precious healing and use your praise to combat any additional attacks from the enemy.

God is faithful. Trust Him to surface and remove those things in your life that are keeping you from full service to Him and those around you. Trust that it's not about anything you can do. It rests not in your abilities, talents, words, or gifts. It rests only on Him and through Him. Keep your eyes focused on God and obey the charge He gives you knowing He'll bring it to pass through His power and for His glory.

> **God is faithful.**

Caroline Klug

▛ Then you will call, and the Lord will answer; you will cry for help, and He will say: Here am I. Isaiah 58:9

Release | The Call to Persevere

> Consider it pure joy, my brothers, whenever
> you face trials of many kinds, because you
> know that the testing of your faith develops
> perseverance. Perseverance must finish its
> work so that you may be mature and
> complete, not lacking anything.
> James 1:2-4

Every day, people all over the world ask the age-old question of whether or not God makes bad things happen. I'm here to give you the answer – absolutely not. To understand this question in its entirety, we have to recognize two things. The first is that there's a distinct difference between what God causes to happen and what He allows. The second has to do with our own, often misguided, interpretation of good and bad.

Although we've highlighted the beginning of Chapter 1, we can't miss the passage in the middle. James 1:13 tells us God doesn't tempt us, "but each one is tempted when, by his own evil desire, he is dragged away and enticed." God may be sovereign, but He also gave us a free will. When we go in a direction that's not scripturally sound or not what God called us to, we open doors to effects and consequences that can be unpleasant.

Caroline Klug

If we're honest with ourselves, we can probably admit that many of the painful things we experience are the direct result of decisions we chose to make outside of God's direction.

However great our mistakes, there are also times we find ourselves in situations where we have no control – situations where we are simply found hurting as the result of an unexpected tragedy, such as death, which is all too familiar to me. I lost my dad when I was twenty-one and my oldest brother when I was thirty-two, both unexpectedly. There are never words to describe the grief. This is just one example. Some get news of a loved one's terminal illness. Another of their child being crippled in an accident. Yet another that their job was eliminated. These are the days we wake up and realize what happened the day before really wasn't just a bad dream, but an excruciatingly painful reality that hit us like the train we never saw coming. What then? Let's look at what James goes on to say in 1:17. He tells us all good things come from the Father above. It's no coincidence James uses these words to follow the others. If the Word tells us all good things come from God, and we know the Word is truth we can stand on, then we have to acknowledge that God isn't standing up in heaven looking for ways to bring hurt into our lives. We know Satan takes care of that part (Job 1:7, 1 Peter 5:8). What God does, however, is allow certain pains to come our way or use natural tragedies or the consequences of another's actions as a means to strengthen us and teach us to lean on Him. James is telling us although we may face trials of many kinds, God allows them for our good. He allows them as a means to create character and a faith that can persevere within the fire (1

The Waiting Room

Peter 1:3-7). This may not seem like consolation when we're hurting, but if we trust who God is, then we can trust He's got our back no matter what happens – even when we don't feel it. There's a reason for everything. We have to find peace with the fact that we may never know what those reasons are until we're sharing a banquet table with Christ.

This brings us to the definitions of *good* and *bad* that we cling to. One of the amazing mysteries of our God is that He's able to take something tragic and turn it into a heart and life transforming event for His glory (Romans 8:28). When we can come to a place where we truly trust God and believe He is love, then we know we can persevere through the things that seem *bad* and do all things through Christ who strengthens us. When we persevere, we are persisting in an idea or task despite obstacles. We are enduring, despite whatever may stand in the way of that purpose. When you make up your mind to trust God and know, despite the pain, He allowed it for a higher purpose, God can take what Satan intended to harm you with and use it to bring glory to His Kingdom.

I was very close to my dad. His death was a severe and unexpected blow to me. Faith was a central part of who he was, and he spent a lot of time planting those seeds of faith with me. After his death, I was angry with God for a long time, feeling as though God took him from me too soon. I let my anger

> **God can take what Satan intended to harm you with and use it to bring glory to His Kingdom.**

put up a wall and it was the catalyst which started a fear of abandonment that took me more than a decade to heal from. Now that I'm through the storm, it's much easier for me to look back and see where God was at work, using all things for the good. I still miss my dad very much, but I can recognize that God used that event in a pretty powerful way to force me to ask questions and walk down a path that would ultimately secure my choice to have a real relationship with Jesus.

Grief has its rightful place in the process of healing. Nothing takes that away but time. What rises above the grief is an assurance that God has a plan for all things. After I learned of the tragic loss of my brother, God comforted me saying, "It is not about what you can handle, but what you let Me carry." May all our pains be a gateway for God's glory. Praise Him in your storm.

> ◼ You intended to harm me, but God intended it for good to accomplish what is now being done, the saving of many lives.
> Genesis 50:20

Release | The Climb Upward

> "I took you from the ends of the earth, from its
> farthest corners I called you. I said, 'You are
> my servant'; I have chosen you and have not
> rejected you. So do not fear, for I am with
> you; do not be dismayed, for I am your God.
> I will strengthen you and help you; I will
> uphold you with my righteous right hand."
> Isaiah 41:9-10

In the book of Exodus, we learn of Moses' call to lead God's people out of their bondage in Egypt, and out from under the hand of the Pharaoh (Exodus 3-4). At this time in his life, Moses and his family had settled near Mount Horeb, southeast of the Mediterranean Sea. While tending the flocks, Moses saw a bush fire burning on top of Mount Horeb. It wasn't just any bush fire. The one he was looking at didn't seem to consume the branches. Moses set his mind to see what this wonder was about. On entering the presence of the fire, God spoke to him, saying, "Do not come any closer. Take off your sandals, for the place where you are standing is holy ground" (Exodus 3:5). As you read through the remaining verses, God makes His plan and calling clear to Moses, giving him signs and wonders of assurance that He would go before Moses in this great journey – the next mountain he was to climb.

I find it interesting that Moses, quite literally, had to climb a mountain in order to see the burning bush. This feels like a foreshadowing of the spiritual mountain God placed in front of him. In its simplest terms, a mountain is an elevated place. God is calling us to a higher level. He's asking us to climb, by faith, to something we can't see until we're there. He may give us a glimpse of what we are climbing toward, but it's not until we reach that level that our perspective can accurately take shape. Imagine a wooden beam, standing lengthwise on top of a large mountain of dirt. As we look upward from the base, our perception might tell us the beam is very tall. However, once at the top, when our perspective is level with the beam, we may find it's not as tall as we originally thought. How often have we looked upward at our own personal mountains, terrified of how large the giant at the top seems, as well as the journey to get there?

> **He's asking us to climb, by faith, to something we can't see until we're there.**

So often, our perceptions of our mountains place fear within us that cause us to turn back. When we turn tail and run, we're missing the glory of our God. The burning bush on Mount Horeb represented that very glory. The Hebrew word for Horeb is *Choreb* (*kho-rabe'*), the root of which actually means desolate. Moses had no other reason to climb what he knew to be a desolate place, other than the fire that burned, calling him to what he would soon find was the presence of God. God wants you to see that as you journey up your mountain one step at a time, it's for a higher purpose. You may be

The Waiting Room

afraid of what you see. You may think you don't have the will to take the steps necessary to follow the leading He's placed in your heart, but trust that God knows what you don't. He knows the very desires of your heart. His intent for those who follow Him is to give them life to the fullest (John 10:10). He knows that, however terrifying the surrendering of your perceptions are, there is a much greater reward waiting. Cling to the signs and wonders He's already given you. Hold fast to what He's already spoken in your spirit. These things are there as your assurance, to guide you and give you strength in the journey.

God may lead you to what seems like a desolate place. Be confident in this: when you make the climb through obedience and faith, He'll meet you there with His glory, and you'll find joy immeasurable.

> The thief comes only to steal and kill and destroy; I have come that they may have life, and have it to the full. *John 10:10*

Caroline Klug

ʀᴇʟᴇᴀsᴇ | Surrender

> Then Jesus said to His disciples, "Whoever wants to be My disciple must deny themselves and take up their cross and follow me. For whoever wants to save their life will lose it, but whoever loses their life for me will find it."
> Matthew 16:24-45

I imagine the title alone may have sent waves of discomfort through you. It sure did to me for a number of years. As Christians, we like to sing about surrender, but walking that talk is a lot harder than it sounds on Sunday morning. If we look to Merriam-Webster to help us define *surrender*, we find the following:

"a: to yield to the power, control, or possession of another or b: to give up completely or agree to forgo especially in favor of another."

When we surrender to God, we're giving Him authority to exercise His sovereign judgment in our lives. To clarify, this isn't God overruling our ability to have free will. It's us giving to God what we *think* is best, in return for what He *knows* is best.

Caroline Klug

If you have kids, particularly teenagers, then you're well aware of a thing I like to call the "Omni Effect." The Omni Effect is the result of a child turning the age at which they know the answer to every question ever asked. They no longer need the wisdom of their parents because they're smarter and far wiser in the ways of the world, despite experiencing only a fraction of what their parents have. They know what's best, so they feel they should be able to do what they like. They believe the world has changed so dramatically, that we, as parents, couldn't possibly be smart enough to guide and educate them. Are you parents out there rolling your eyes yet? I thought so. This is a pretty easy concept for us to grasp, right? What if we applied this to our all-knowing God? News flash: *we* are those kids. We're the ones who have experienced only a fraction of what God has. I don't think we could even call it a fraction. That would be far too generous. He knows all because He created all. The Bible tells us every day was written before one of them came to be (Psalm 139:16). He's the only One able to provide perfect guidance in perfect timing.

> **Surrender is giving to God what we *think* is best, in return for what He *knows* is best.**

Perhaps the greatest testimony of surrender happens when we, amidst the charge of the enemy, lay down our shield, get on our knees, and lift our hands. It's not a white flag we hold, but the offering of our will to God, whatever the outcome may be. To give yourself wholly and completely to the will of God, without regard to your own personal desires, is the epitome of surrender. It's also terrifying.

The Waiting Room

Why is it so scary? Why is there fear in surrender? We fall into the trap of fear when one of two things happen. The first is we believe the lies of the enemy. Satan doesn't want you to be close to God. In fact, he wants nothing but misery and death for you (John 10:10). He's going to whisper lies into your ear about why what God wants for you isn't going to make you happy. He's going to stir confusion and doubt. There's a way to combat that. Fall on the Word. God has not given us a spirit of fear, but a spirit of power, love, and sound mind (2 Timothy 1:7). Search the Scriptures on what God has to say about your situation and who He created you to be.

The second reason we fall into fear is because we don't know, or choose not to rely on, the character of our God. Do you know Him well enough to know He loves you beyond measure (Ephesians 3:17-19); that He, Himself is love (1 John 4:8)? Do you trust His heart enough to know He longs to bless you and give you every good thing (Psalm 37:4, Matthew 7:9-11)? It's impossible for God to lie and it's impossible for God to do anything outside the character of goodness. For these reasons, you can trust Him completely.

It's a spiritual truth that you can never out-give God. If God's asking you to give Him something, don't place such a high value on it and cling to it for fear of losing the joy or security you think it brings. When you surrender it to God, you'll find He returns something of even greater value. As I've often told my daughter, doing what's asked of us isn't the extent of obedience. God desires our right attitudes as well. The attitude of surrender should be one of prostration in the presence of an all-knowing God, comforted in the assurance that He knows what you don't. He'll only ask of you what He knows will ultimately lead to both your blessing and His glory. In keeping with our spiritual truth, God will never ask you for something and then return something less than you gave to Him.

Surrendering doesn't make you weak. It's what you do when you *are* weak, so God can be your strength. However difficult this may be for you, take your treasure – your money, time, job, relationship, food, home, hobbies, whatever He's asking for – and lay it at His feet. He'll return what you never thought possible, including freedom. Don't be bound in slavery to the things you refuse to let go of out of fear. It's keeping you from a greater blessing and a beautiful display of His Glory.

▞ Take delight in the LORD, and He will give you the desires of your heart. Psalm 37:4

The Waiting Room

Release | Cut the Ropes

> Then Paul said to the centurion and the
> soldiers, "Unless these men stay with the ship,
> you cannot be saved." So the soldiers cut the
> ropes that held the lifeboat and let it drift away.
> Acts 27: 31-32

For Paul, living a life of reckless abandon required his utmost trust and certainty in God. It required an attentive ear and a heart open to the continual leading of God's Spirit. Along the way, God used Paul as a vessel to extend His grace to those around him. Today, let's set sail for Italy, and ask ourselves if we have what it takes to cut the ropes.

While Paul was in Syria, he was warned by the prophet, Agabus, that Jewish leaders would arrest him and turn him over to the Gentiles. When the other disciples heard this, they urged Paul not to continue on to Jerusalem. Paul was strong in the Lord and determined in his mission. Despite the warnings from his brothers, he moved on to Jerusalem. While in the temple, a group of Jews created an uprising against him. They made false accusations, claiming Paul brought Greeks into their temple which, in their eyes, would have defiled it. Paul was seized by the crowd. What transpires next would take a book to truly do it justice – an amazing story in and of itself. For our purposes today, I'll summarize by saying Paul was indicted and brought before Felix (the Roman Procurator), the Sanhedrin, then Festus (the Judean Procurator), then to King Agrippa, who finally granted his appeal to Caesar, in Rome.

They were to sail to Italy along with several other prisoners: 276 souls in total. Winds and weather were not cooperating and when they were near Crete, Paul warned the men of impending disaster to the ship, its cargo, and themselves if they were to continue onward. Rather than listen to Paul, the centurion in charge took his orders from the ship's captain and continued forward. Scripture tells us they soon began to encounter hurricane-force winds and were forced to give way to them, allowing the storm to govern them helplessly. After the weather-related tragedies we've seen here in the United States, and off the shores of our great nation, the vision of severity should take on new meaning for each of us. Paul records they couldn't keep the lifeboat secure, and needed to bring it on board, wrapping ropes around it to keep the lifeboat itself in one piece. The storm became so fierce, they were forced to throw the cargo overboard. After several life-threatening days, those on board gave up hope of being saved.

It was at this point Paul stood and addressed them. This was not a quiet congregation at the temple. This was a huge vessel in the middle of a full-on hurricane. I have to believe Paul would have needed to shout at the top of his lungs just to overpower the sound of the wind and waves, and the crashing and creaking of wood as the ship took hit after merciless hit from the sea. At this point it

The Waiting Room

says they had not eaten in a long time. I have to assume they were also sleep-deprived and drenched to the skin. This scene reeks of agitation and desperation – not likely a crowd willing to listen. Given this, I would say Paul was pretty gutsy, as he started his address with words that sounded like an "I told you so" (Acts 27:21). It must have been the grace of God which kept the men in check, allowing him to continue on to the good part. Paul tells them, "… not one of you will be lost. Only the ship will be destroyed. Last night an angel of the God to whom I belong and whom I serve stood beside me and said, 'Do not be afraid, Paul. You must stand trial before Caesar; and God has graciously given you the lives of all who sail with you.' So keep your courage, men, for I have faith in God that it will happen just as He told me." (Acts 27:22-25)

I can only imagine the thoughts and fears which struck the hearts of the other 275 souls on board – all caught between the hope of something bigger than themselves and the terror of the reality before their eyes. Who is this man who speaks of supernatural rescue? What about him causes me to take hold of his words and believe? Although the answers to those questions were not evident to most of them, they could likely be summed up in one word – grace.

However, not all on board were keen on the plan. As the storm continued to drive them across the Adriatic Sea, it seems they reached a point when fears peaked and desperation ensued. Allow me to explain why I believe it was desperation. Remember the lifeboat the crew hauled on board and tied ropes around to keep in one piece? It says a few of the people decided a better plan would be to lower that lifeboat back into the water and escape in it. They even hatched a plan to do it under false pretenses, saying they were lowering anchors instead. The minute we qualify anything with a falsehood, this should be an instant indication of our conviction over what we're about to do, and a warning fire to, pun intended, abandon ship.

As I sit cozily at Starbucks with my hot coffee nearby, it's not difficult for me to look on as an outsider and know these men have completely lost their marbles. They're in the middle of a hurricane and want to lower a boat a fraction of the size and protection of the one they're currently on, which was initially getting ripped apart and had to be held together with ropes. Oh, and they want to *get in* this boat. Need I say more? Paul sees what's going on and tells the centurion if the men leave the ship, they'll be killed. What happens next is the lone verse in this entire story which left me speechless. It says, "So the soldiers cut the ropes that held the lifeboat and let it drift away" (Acts 27:32). Imagine the gravity of this scene – the terror of the storm engulfing them as they shout across the open deck, clinging to anything of substance to keep from being thrown overboard into the raging sea. There is one hand fiercely gripping the rope to the lifeboat while the other grips the starboard of the ship. Which to let go of and which to cling to?

> **Sometimes choosing life means you have a lifeboat you need to cut the ropes on.**

A life or death decision.

Sometimes choosing life means you have a lifeboat you need to cut the ropes on – the Plan B you concoct

The Waiting Room

when you don't think what God spoke to your heart is possible. Questioning what you see can lead you into moments of desperation and cause you to make plans which lead outside His protection and far from His blessings. Take the leading we're so graciously given here – don't just haul your lifeboat back up on deck. Stand in faith and cut the ropes on it. Remember, God's greatest glory comes from situations where we can't see a clear answer. It is then He does what we never imagined possible.

▪ ... everyone reached land safely.
Acts 27:44

Caroline Klug

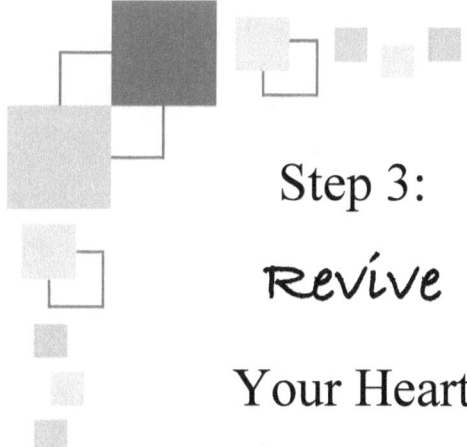

Step 3: Revive Your Heart

So far, we've reminded our hearts of who God is and the importance of what He's doing during our wait. We've released our hearts to Him, trusting that He who does all things for the good (Romans 8:28) will meet our needs how and when He alone knows is best. Now it's time to revive our hearts.

Merriam-Webster defines the word revive as meaning "to restore from a depressed, inactive, or unused state; to bring back." I love this definition so much. It's filled with hope. Loved one, I know you might be tired. You might be feeling like you're in that depressed or inactive state, but when you make the decision to release your heart and all your troubles to the Holy of Holies, He can turn your sorrow into joy and your mourning into dancing (Psalm 30:11-12). He can take you from an unused state and bring you back to a place where you can move mountains.

As you continue into this next section, here are a few things you can do and keep in mind, to continue forward with that right perspective during your wait.

Cut the Ropes... No, Really

Remember those lifeboats we talked about? Those Plan B's in case God didn't come through? If you have any still hanging around somewhere, now is the time to cut the ropes on them. I know it's hard, but you'll never be able to pick up the gift He wants to give you if you're still hanging on to the one that was never intended for you. I should know. I wrote the book on that one, (literally) as you'll read about in an upcoming chapter, titled "Ten Years."

Did you know the journey from Egypt to the Promised Land was roughly 250 miles? This should have taken the Israelites forty days, not forty years. I'm guessing those lifeboats they were lugging behind them through the sand were pretty big and heavy to cause that kind of a delay.

Think Good Thoughts

Proverbs 15:15 says, "All the days of the oppressed are wretched, but the cheerful heart has a continual feast." For those of us with teenagers, it's evident when they are brooding over something. They go in their rooms, close the door and listen to the most depressing songs they can find in their playlists. If we're honest with ourselves, we can have a tendency to do the same thing. All this does is feed the brooding and send us to an even darker place. It's the complete opposite of what this verse in Proverbs is trying to teach us.

God does things to help our hurting hearts, but sometimes *we* need to take some ownership. If you're feeling down, don't lock yourself in your room and listen to "Hurt" by Nine Inch Nails. Instead, try playing some praise and worship music, or whatever your favorite happy tunes are, and see what happens. If you really want to get crazy, SING to those happy songs. Do you know how hard it is to stay mad or sad when you're singing happy songs? Joy is much more powerful than sadness. If you choose to set your mind on things that are good then, little by little, that joy will overtake the darkness and you'll find yourself in a completely different frame of mind. I dare you to try it.

Believe in the God of the Impossible

Few things can empower our spiritual walks as greatly as seeing one of our mountains be moved. But I also believe few things can excite God more than seeing one of His children *believe* He can move the mountain *before* He moves it.

God promised Abraham descendants as numerous as the stars (Genesis 15:5). By the time Abraham was 100 years old, he faced the fact that his body was "as good as dead" because of his age, but yet he still believed "against all hope" that God would do as He promised and he gave glory to God for it (Romans 4:18-21). The thought of having a baby at 100 years old sounds more like a nightmare than a dream to me, but considering he lived to the ripe age of 175, I guess we'll call that a win. The important thing here is that Abraham had no physical or earthly reason to believe God would give him descendants too numerous to count. What he did have reason to believe in was the character and the capabilities of the God who made him that promise. Don't let your time in the waiting room be burdened by fear or doubt. If He spoke it, so shall it be.

Be Watchful

What kind of a difference would it make in our spiritual walks if we could stop *waiting* for God and start *watching* for Him instead?

The act of waiting isn't so much an act at all. It's something much more passive. It implies staying where we are and taking no action. When I picture someone waiting, I think about them sitting patiently in the waiting room with their hands folded in their lap, maybe thumbing through an old magazine to pass the time. On the flip side, watching has a very different implication to it. Now we're talking about something that's active. I'll go one step further and say it's something *pro*active.

What's happening in your spirit while you're in the waiting room? Are you thumbing through old magazines or are you focused on the receptionist desk, watching for any signs of you being next? This might be a silly example but, the reality is, God gives you signs and wonders all around you that He's working on your behalf. If you're watching for them, you'll see them. You'll be encouraged and revived by them. You'll see the folder with your name on it being pulled from the rack and opened up.

The Waiting Room

Seeing those signs will give you energy to keep on going and keep on waiting a little longer if you have to. You may not always know what you're looking for, but you sure know *Who* you're looking for.

Remember – before God can revive your heart, you'll have to cut the ropes on any Plan B you might have. Keep your thoughts positive and fed with positive influences. Believe in the God of the impossible. Be watchful for Him and open to the signs He's trying to encourage your heart with. Open the eyes of your heart.

Caroline Klug

The Waiting Room

Revive | Moving Mountains

> Jesus replied, "I tell you the truth, if you have faith and do not doubt, not only can you do what was done to the fig tree, but also you can say to this mountain, 'Go, throw yourself into the sea,' and it will be done."
> Matthew 21:21

My husband Jim and I once went hiking in the Jemez Mountains, near Albuquerque, NM. Part of the drive there was through holes excavated through the mountainside. It was pure rock around us. Talk about feeling small. And slightly afraid. Standing in awe of the enormity of that mountain made me realize just how big a statement Jesus was making when He told us we could tell a mountain to throw itself into the sea. It made me realize just how much He wanted us to grasp how powerful faith can be if we stop our minds from getting in the way. There are several places in the Bible where God tells us to remember Him as the father of Abraham, Isaac, and Jacob. He's reminding us that the same God who did amazing things in the lives of these men is the same God today and forever (Hebrews 13:8). Because of that, we know the same power at work when Jesus withered that fig tree is the same power alive and well within each of us as believers and followers of Christ. Our mission, should we choose to accept it, is to move mountains.

People question how literally we should take some of these passages. I imagine our beginning Scripture falls under particular scrutiny, as the task suggested would be quite a tremendous feat, both for our physical bodies and in wrapping our tiny human brains around how this could be possible. There are several places in the Bible where an open and obvious use of parables or analogies occurs. Let me stand out on my somewhat lonely ledge and say that I don't believe this is one of them.

In this particular instance, based on the words and actions of Jesus, we have more reason to believe Jesus was serious about being able to move mountains than not. I believe we're supposed to take what Jesus said quite literally. In the account written by Matthew, we learn Jesus withered a fig tree, which was directly witnessed by the disciples. This was not an analogy, a parable, or a metaphor. It simply happened. Why would Jesus give a literal demonstration of the fig tree and then follow that up with something not intended to be taken seriously?

I hate to point out the obvious, but the disciples were not exactly Rhodes Scholars. On several occasions Jesus had to explain His parables to them separately after teaching a crowd. I believe Jesus used this fig tree very strategically as an opportunity to demonstrate the very real and tangible power available for those who believe.

So how do we get from believing small things like the line at Starbucks moving faster, to big things like hurtling mountains? In order to have a faith that turns the unexpected into the expected, we need to develop an

The Waiting Room

understanding of the One our faith depends on – the One whose power alone moves those mountains. We need to build a relationship with the power source and dive into His Word to understand what we can plug into. Once we're plugged in, we have a constant energy source to draw from. It's a source that will fuel our faith and motivate our will to believe. To know God is to know infinite possibilities.

I know I just made that sound easy. It's not. Logic and physics wage war against our puny minds. It's easier to retreat to the comfort of what we know is possible versus the discomfort of trying to rationalize what seems impossible. Changing this is daily work, and we need to ask God for help to build in us a faith to move mountains. He would never offer us something He wasn't serious about giving.

With all that said, I think there's an additional message in this Scripture. I absolutely believe we can take Jesus literally here, but I also believe He's telling us to look beyond the mountain to the everyday things we are believing Him for – believing Him for answers to our prayers, or the fulfillment of something He spoke to your heart that seems impossible or outside your grasp. If throwing a mountain is possible, then so is whatever He's talking to your heart about, no matter how big or intimidating it seems. You've heard the saying, "It's not black and white." Well, sometimes it *is* black and white. Either you believe, or you don't.

> **God doesn't change, so why should our faith?**

The power that withered the fig tree is the same power that gave life to the resurrected body of Christ. It's this same power that will transform your circumstances and

Caroline Klug

bring about the result of whatever it is God is asking you to believe for. God doesn't change, so why should our faith? God is not on the Throne intermittently. He was, is, and will be there forever. His power will never be equaled, and His Name will never be surpassed. Choose this day who you will serve (Joshua 24:15). And believe.

> But when he asks, he must believe and not doubt, because he who doubts is like a wave of the sea, blown and tossed by the wind. That man should not think he will receive anything from the Lord. James 1:6-7

The Waiting Room

Revive | Great Expectations

> "This is what the Lord says— Israel's King and
> Redeemer, the Lord Almighty: I am the first
> and I am the last; apart from Me there is no
> God. Who then is like Me? Let him proclaim it.
> Let him declare and lay out before Me what has
> happened since I established My ancient
> people, and what is yet to come— yes, let him
> foretell what will come. Do not tremble, do
> not be afraid. Did I not proclaim this and
> foretell it long ago? You are My witnesses.
> Is there any God besides Me? No, there is no
> other Rock; I know not one."
> Isaiah 44:6-8

All too often, we're faced with the harsh ways reality falls short of our expectations. We step up to the plate, brush the dust off our big ideas, and find the people or situations we depended on couldn't or wouldn't come through. These encounters repeatedly render us wounded, and we act as if we're surprised by the stunning blow. Eventually, our wounds cause complacency and we stop expecting anything more than disappointment. We lose the motivation that once sparked our dreams and we accept mediocrity as our standard. If this is you, lift your eyes to the hills and understand that, with God, your standard can exceed any expectation you can dare to dream.

Sometimes we try to rely on our own abilities, or the abilities of others, to advance our need or promote our sense of worth. We rely on the people of our inner circles for security and assurance. I've learned the hard way that people will always disappoint you on some level. People are flawed. The higher you hold someone or something in your life, the more it will hurt when it all comes hurtling down. As you painfully make your way through the rubble, there is One who is watching you. There is One who is aching for you to cry out to Him for help. It's the One whose place is in the highest of realms and on the strongest of foundations that will never be shaken. Afforded to us through our relationship with Christ is the miracle-working power of God. It's time to brush off the lies and the doubt and really understand Who is working on your behalf.

> **With God, your standard can exceed any expectation you can dare to dream.**

I'm not talking about an exceptional prophet or an extraordinary person. I'm talking about a supernatural God. Let what I'm about to say sink in. As a Christ follower, you are a child of the King. As a child of the King, you are granted the intimate privilege of entering the Throne room. Anytime. Anywhere. When was the last time you entered into the secret place of His majestic Throne room, and worshipped Him for His awesome power? Have you stopped to consider all that His hands have made, and all that His knowledge has willed into existence? By a power that is so foreign to us and so far

The Waiting Room

beyond our reach, all things are possible for him who believes (Mark 9:23). Nowhere in Scripture does it say all things are possible for him who takes things into his own hands.

We spend an obnoxious amount of energy on worrying, analyzing, and trying to come up with solutions to our problems. If we spent a quarter of that time on our knees in worship to the One who can actually do something about it, I'm convinced we would all be spiritual generations ahead of where we are. I'm not exempt from this struggle. I just recently found myself in an emotional situation where I was trying to assume control of something I had no business controlling. It was painful, but I had to go before God for forgiveness, and completely release it and walk away from it. Once I did that, I was mercifully reminded of how wonderful it is to let go of what burdened my heart and know it was in much more capable hands. Believing God for the best outcome is not always easy in our flesh, but it's the only thing that makes sense in the light of who He is.

Our God is the master suspense writer. Through His Word, He's given us a history of events that unfold against the toughest of odds and the most impossible of situations. Expect the unexpected and you'll never be disappointed. When you think about something in the context of knowing God is involved, all bets are off. It means what you perceive as real may not be, and what you perceive as impossible is merely a door for God's glory to shine through.

Recognize the power at work, and that it's not of your hands but of the all-powerful, all-sufficient God Almighty. While you are in the waiting room, a wonderful way to praise and honor God is by waiting with great expectations. Let your faith be seen by the expectations of your heart.

> He who forms the mountains, creates the wind, and reveals His thoughts to man, He who turns dawn to darkness, and treads the high places of the earth— the Lord God Almighty is His name. *Amos 4:13*

The Waiting Room

Revive | Dry Bones (Part 1)

The hand of the Lord was on me, and He
brought me out by the Spirit of the Lord and set
me in the middle of a valley; it was full of
bones. He led me back and forth among them,
and I saw a great many bones on the floor of
the valley, bones that were very dry. He asked
me, "Son of man, can these bones live?" I said,
"O Sovereign Lord, You alone know."
Ezekiel 37:1-3

Do you believe God has the ability to take what's dead and breathe life into the very core of it? Do you believe God has the ability to change who a person is from the very inside out? Nothing is hopeless. No one is a lost cause. There's a message burning in me, and I pray it impacts your heart and mind in a way that changes your life and the lives of those around you. I'm going to say it again. Nothing is hopeless, and no one is a lost cause. What do you have in your life that looks like these dry bones? Is it your marriage? Your health? Your job? The salvation of your child? Some of you might feel like these dry bones represent your whole life. In Part 1 and Part 2, I'd like to

> **Nothing is hopeless. No one is a lost cause.**

talk about two things – what we're allowing God to do in our lives and what we're believing Him for in the lives of those we know and love. Like all good life practices, we'll focus first on what we do have control over – ourselves.

Our verse is out of the Old Testament and centers on a vision given to the prophet Ezekiel. God had previously placed a judgment on Israel for her sin. The Spirit of God takes Ezekiel and shows him a valley of dry bones representing Israel's hopeless condition in exile. God gives Ezekiel direction to prophesy over the bones and, through the breath of God, these bones stand and become a vast army. I get goosebumps even writing that. I could tangent into an entire writing on how stunning the vision of those bones coming to life would be, but I'll save that for another time. The simple point being made here is that God has the ability to take what is dead and rotting and bring it standing at attention, full of life.

What's the practical application here? Getting to know God. You can't believe in someone's abilities unless you spend some time getting to know them. I recommend two simple approaches. Spend time with Him and spend time with people who know and love Him. Anyone who spends time reading the Bible and studying the character of God learns who He is and what He's capable of. God assured us we would have trials in this world. In that same breath, He also assured us He's already overcome the one who is of the world – the enemy (John 16:33). Learn and ask questions. God is big enough to handle your toughest questions. Spending time with people who already have a relationship with Him is a great way to learn and be encouraged. Mature Christians

The Waiting Room

can also help you navigate your questions by aligning them with what the Bible says.

Learning and believing is only half the battle. Once we learn who He is and what He's about, we have to make the choice to put God in the driver's seat and allow Him to use His power to change us and our circumstances. We could be here for days debating why we should give control of our lives over to God. For the sake of time, I'll put it as simply as my heart has learned to. God is on the Throne – period. He placed every star in the sky. He placed our earth on its axis. He has brought everything and everyone into existence from the creation of time. Through His Word, His prophets, and His signs, He has predicted every moment of this world since before any of those moments came into being. There's nothing that escapes His view or His control. There's no thought within your mind or desire within your heart that escapes His attention. With that said, ask yourself something. If our God who did all this, and is all this, knows your every desire and need, should you have any doubt when believing in Him to fulfill those desires and needs?

I understand, intimately, transformation can be painful. It's scary enough to admit what our shortcomings are, but once we see them, we have to make a choice. We can either remain in the place we are currently, knowing those shortcomings are causing us pain, or we can believe in the God I described above to change us from the "heart-side" out. It's frightening to give ourselves over to change, but

> **Allow God to change you from the "heart-side" out.**

you can trust God is in complete control and would never do anything short of your best interest. As much as I know the pain, I also know the joy and amazing reward it brings to walk in that transformation. When God lives in you, He leaves peace where there was unrest and healing where there was hurt. I can guarantee you won't come out the same person. I can also guarantee you won't miss the person you leave behind.

The Maker of Heaven and earth breathed life into you when you were created. If you seek Him and allow Him in, He can breathe that new life into you again, for salvation or the breath of saving grace to pull you through your trials. He is more than able. Seek Him. Trust Him. Invite Him. Don't wait another second. What are you still doing here? [Smile]

> ...In this world you will have trouble. But take heart! I have overcome the world.
> John 16:33

Revive | Dry Bones (Part 2)

> The hand of the Lord was on me, and He
> brought me out by the Spirit of the Lord and set
> me in the middle of a valley; it was full of
> bones. He led me back and forth among them,
> and I saw a great many bones on the floor of
> the valley, bones that were very dry. He asked
> me, "Son of man, can these bones live?" I said,
> "O Sovereign Lord, You alone know."
> Ezekiel 37:1-3

In Part 1, I shared a message that nothing is hopeless, and no one is a lost cause. God can take a valley of dry bones and raise them into a living and breathing army with one small breath. In an earlier chapter, we talked about the life-transforming power of God within our own lives when we take the step to invite Him in and believe. Today we'll focus on what you're believing Him for, as you pray for change in the lives of those you know and love.

Praying for God-honoring change in the life of another is part of our job description as Christians. However, this can be a slippery slope. The minute we start passing judgment on people around us, we're entering into sin ourselves. I've seen many people throw their hands up at Christianity because they feel rejection rather than the love of Christ from people who are supposed to be the example. They ask themselves, "If this is what it means to be a Christian, why would I want to be one of those?" As Christians, we're called to love. The judgment seat belongs to God alone. I'm not here to say my attitude is always perfect, but God has blessed me with a deep understanding of a truth I'm resigned to remember. John Bradford, English Reformer from the 1500s, coined the phrase appropriately when he said, "If not for the grace of God, there go I."

I know who I was. I know the sin that has been in my own life. I also know I'm human and still stumble from time to time. The mere fact that I'm not perfect tells me I have sin in my life. I'm guessing you're in the same boat. We have no right to look at anyone around us and judge them. Our job is to allow God to change us, and to love and pray for the people around us. Now that that's out of the way, let's talk about how we can use that right attitude to be a blessing to others.

I have a deep respect for my daughter's grandmother. She was a mother to me for many years and was one of the key individuals who led me to Christ. She's an amazing woman with unbelievable wisdom, from whom I learned countless things. One of those things has been the power of prayer. Early in my walk with God, I recall listening to her pray, and wondering how I would ever learn to use words and Scripture like that. She taught me that prayer is less about using the right words and more about building a relationship with God, speaking to Him from the heart, and believing He is at the very center of every moment with me. How amazed

The Waiting Room

would we be if we really knew what transpired in the spiritual realm, and how would that propel us forward in urgent prayer for the people around us? God is at the center. He hears our prayers and is working on our behalf. When you pray for help and blessings for someone else, those prayers are being set in action. Sometimes we see results immediately, and sometimes it takes several years before we see them come to pass in a visible way. Regardless, your prayers are shaking Kingdom foundations.

A powerful way we can pray for others is through the use of the Scriptures and hymns God gave us. God is the only one who is all-knowing, and the only one who can know with certainty what the right thing is for someone else. When we pray the promises of Scripture over someone else, we're guaranteed to be praying God's will over them. It's a powerful way to ensure positive prayer while keeping our own selfish motivations out of our requests. If you have someone in your life who you think needs to change, rather than asking God to change that specific characteristic, try asking God to bring them closer to Him and grow in them a knowledge, wisdom, and love for God. When you do that, those other things will naturally come under the scope of God's transformation, and in the timing He alone knows is best. Let God be the judge of what needs to change in someone else, and when. That keeps us out of the judgment seat, which belongs to God.

> **When we pray the promises of Scripture, we're guaranteed to be praying God's will.**

Caroline Klug

Remember the dry bones from the beginning of this chapter? Spend some devoted time asking God to breathe life into those bones in a way that honors Him. Choose to be positive about your prayers and have a spirit of anticipation of God's response. Pray blessings over those bones out loud. Proverbs 18:21 tells us the power of life and death rest in the words we speak. God is telling us to speak life. He's telling us to believe He can do all things, in ourselves and in the lives of those around us. If you pray God's biblical promises over yourself and others, you can rest in complete faith that He will follow through.

🔲 The tongue has the power of life and death, and those who love it will eat its fruit.
Proverbs 18:21

Revive | Let Nothing Move You

> But thanks be to God! He gives us the victory
> through our Lord Jesus Christ. Therefore,
> my dear brothers, stand firm. Let nothing move
> you. Always give yourself fully to the work
> of the Lord, because you know that your
> labor in the Lord is not in vain.
> 1 Corinthians 15:57-58

In all things God is right next to you in your struggles, in total and complete control, and holding back the things He knows would be too much for you. Your God doesn't set people up for failure. He brings victory to all who will call on His name and stand firm in His truth. Our victory in our struggles has everything to do with how willing we are to take our stand firmly and confidently in Christ. The key word here is *stand*. We rarely recognize we've been given the easy part of the battle.

There's a show that used to be on television years ago called Fear Factor. Contestants on the show would face all things frightening, from high-speed crashes to being buried alive. If they endured to the end, they would win a large sum of money. As I meditated on our beginning Scripture, I found my mind drifting to thoughts of this show and, particularly so, the challenges involving bugs.

Picture a person lying down in a glass case as tens, then hundreds, and eventually thousands of bugs begin crawling all over them. They're covered from head to toe and have to endure quite a mental battle as the bugs make their way into their clothes, ears, and nose. Eventually, I have to believe the bugs would start affecting their breathing. For some contestants, all it took was a hundred or so before it would set off a panic that would send them rushing out screaming, with arms flailing. This would definitely be me. For others, I was amazed at the calmness they displayed to the very end. As I thought about this, I realized the mental image God was creating for me. We're all on the battlefield. We're all facing a lot of things that frighten us and challenge what we know to be true. This brings me to my first point concerning truth.

For these contestants, they all had a very strong truth they could choose to hold to. These challenges were not about life and death. Trust me when I say that show had some attorneys hard at work to ensure the challenge would not put a person's life at risk. The bugs they used were not poisonous. This had everything to do with what was going on inside that person's head. Pay close attention to this next insight. The people who gave up early chose to believe the lie that they would be hurt more than the truth that they could not be hurt. It's the same for us. We have the truth of God's Word to hold to. God tells us the battle belongs to Him and He'll fight for us (2 Chronicles 20:15). He tells us that He'll never give us more than we can handle (1 Corinthians 10:13). He tells us all we have to do is put on the armor of God and stand,

The Waiting Room

and He will do the rest (Ephesians 6:13). It's God who will fight on the battlefield for us. We are only required to stand firm.

For us, the battling usually isn't done openly. It's done mentally. I've been through battles that required me to choose every minute of every day what truth I believe. I've been through battles that had so many bugs I felt my airways closing and the panic setting in. Just like the contestants who endured on that show, you must remain calm and allow God's many truths to fill your mind and heart. Whether from it or through it, God will deliver you at the right time.

> **It's God who will fight on the battlefield for us. We are only required to stand firm.**

I want to leave you with an insight I hope you find both powerful and empowering. Our Scripture at the beginning of the chapter points out something very clear if our eyes and minds are open to it. It says, *let* nothing move you. Allow that to sink in for a second. To *let* something implies a choice on our behalf. If we're moved, it's because we let ourselves be moved. Be empowered through Christ to stand firm wherever He needs you to be. Trust that He's already won the battle and the victory. I know the wait isn't easy, especially if it's in the middle of unpleasant circumstances, but His timing is as perfect as His outcomes. Choose this day to stand, and watch God do what you can't.

▄▘ Therefore put on the full armor of God, so that when the day of evil comes, you may be

Caroline Klug

able to stand your ground, and after you have done everything, to stand. Ephesians 6:13

The Waiting Room

Revive | Set Your Mind

> Then he continued, "Do not be afraid, Daniel.
> Since the first day that you set your mind to
> gain understanding and to humble yourself
> before your God, your words were heard, and I
> have come in response to them."
> Daniel 10:12

Did you know your prayers are setting things in motion in the spiritual realm? Did you know there is Scripture to support how literal this is? In reference to our beginning Scripture, the prophet Daniel was praying for understanding of what was to happen to his people. He was about eighty-five years old when God blessed him with a revelation and a visitation from the incarnate (spirit made flesh) Son of God and the angel Gabriel. In exploring Gabriel's message to Daniel, we uncover fascinating revelations about how our faith and prayers contribute to the spiritual battle taking place on our behalf every day.

The visitation opens with Daniel seeing Jesus. The men with Daniel were so frightened by what they saw that every one of them ran away except for Daniel, who was brought to his face and into a deep sleep. At that point, Daniel records he was touched and given enough strength to be brought to his hands and knees. Gabriel proceeds to tell Daniel that he (Daniel) is highly esteemed and that Gabriel has been sent to give him a message. Gabriel tells him, "Do not be afraid, Daniel. Since the first day that you set your mind to gain understanding and to humble yourself before your God, your words were heard, and I have come in response to them. But the prince of the Persian kingdom resisted me twenty-one days. Then Michael, one of the chief princes, came to help me, because I was detained there with the king of Persia" (Daniel 10:12-14).

Without going too deeply, I'd like to help you understand some important biblical context. The prince of the Persian kingdom Gabriel speaks of is not a man, but a spiritual being. Whenever there is reference to Michael, God's archangel, Israel is usually involved somewhere in the equation. Scholars believe that's because Michael has been set as prince over God's chosen nation, to defend and protect her. If Michael is depicted biblically as the strongest angel, it makes sense why God would place him over His beloved Israel.

What do we know about Satan? We know he covets all God has and tries to imitate Him in all things. If God has princes set over nations, so does Satan. The prince of the Persian kingdom who resisted Gabriel was none other than one of Satan's fallen angels. This is a lot to go into for the point I'm making but, trust me, it's an important one. This may be one of the only places in the Bible where we're shown a true glimpse of the spiritual warfare which takes place on our behalf. Gabriel is telling Daniel as soon as he set his mind and humbled himself before God, an answer was given. The reason Daniel didn't see that

The Waiting Room

answer for twenty-one days was because God's angel and Satan's angel were doing spiritual battle.

As a side note, some scholars argue it was only the Son of God present in his vision, but I agree with scholars who say Gabriel had to be present and the one to deliver the message about being detained. For no being, human or spiritual, can detain our Lord.

What moves spiritual battle? Prayer, my friend. Prayer. When Daniel set his mind, he was committing to what he earnestly prayed for. The Hebrew word for set is *nathan* (pronounced naw-than). Some of the words used to define the meaning are commit, doubtless, without fail, fasten, and deliver up. We know from Scripture Daniel was a man of prayer. Knowing that, I assume when Daniel set his mind, he was going to God repeatedly and fervently in prayer.

Why twenty-one days? If God sent Michael to help Gabriel, in order to allow Gabriel to deliver Daniel's answer, why wait three weeks? Why not send Michael right away and get it over with? I've pondered this thought quite a bit. I know you feel weak and uncertain if you can wait any longer for your answer, but take heart. Now is the time to trust God has a very good reason why He's allowing your answer to be detained.

> **God has a very good reason why He's allowing your answer to be detained.**

He may be waiting because of a change that needs to be made in your heart or the heart of another. He may be waiting on a step of obedience He's asked of you. It may only be a test of your faith to see if you'll remain faithful through the wait. There could be a million reasons, but all of them will ultimately be for the good of His Kingdom.

Caroline Klug

Now is the time to set your mind on seeking understanding and direction from your Father and pray passionately to Him. Your prayers are waging war in the spiritual realm. If you believe in God, then you have to believe Satan exists. If you believe that, then you must believe in the world that exists beyond our earthly eyes. Spend time in His Word and know what He says. Search and seek out His Words like the most valuable of commodities, for they are the sword of the Spirit (Ephesians 6:17).

> ...and if you call out for insight and cry aloud for understanding, and if you look for it as for silver and search for it as for hidden treasure, then you will understand the fear of the Lord and find the knowledge of God.
> Proverbs 2:3-5

Revive | Be Watchful

> Devote yourselves to prayer,
> being watchful and thankful.
> Colossians 4:2

We serve an amazing God. Truly. We serve the One who put every star in its place, and named them (Isaiah 40:26, Psalm 147:4). We serve a God who ordained every one of your days before one of them came to be (Psalm 139:16). If we serve a God big enough for such things, then, I ask you, can this same God choose to bring about change, healing, transformation, or anything else He chooses? Undeniably, yes. I'm going to be talking about prayer today, but not the human kind. The God kind. Get ready for a thought transformation.

Prayer is powerful and effective. It's our way to the Father. When you pray with a heart that seeks the will of God, the effects can produce results beyond our comprehension. I'm not talking about the kind of prayers where we're asking to win the lottery. God won't say yes to everything we ask for. He's not a gumball machine. He is sovereign and all-knowing and, if we're going to trust Him, we have to trust His answers are perfectly in line with what will bring ultimate glory to Him and His Kingdom. With that said, the kind of prayer I'm talking about is the kind first inspired by God, where He and He alone is the initiator. Have you ever felt something press on your heart to pray for? Maybe something that wasn't even on your mind to begin with, but God reached out and tugged at your heart strings to place it squarely on your radar? I had an amazing realization not too long ago regarding this type of prayer. It was a simple realization, but one that is forever changing my view of the power of prayer. Let me explain.

It's one thing for us to realize a need and seek God for help. He's faithful and will answer those requests in accordance with His good and perfect will. However, it's something entirely different when God Himself places something on your heart to pray for. Stop and think about this with me for a second. God is asking. He's not responding. He's asking. Would God ever ask you to pray for something He has no intention of actually bringing about? Nothing I have ever read in the Bible about who God is or how He operates would leave me to believe the answer to that question is anything but a resounding no. If *He's* putting it on your heart, you can have absolute faith it's not only in accordance with His will, but something He has every intention of completing. If you don't pray for it, He'll find someone who will. Amen – so shall it be.

I've said it before, and I'll say it again. I can't think of anything more exciting than being part of the army of God. We're on the winning side. His Word tells us the war has already been fought and He's been named Victorious (John 16:33). As flawed human beings, susceptible to our very human emotions, we often run away from trying things we think we'll fail at. We're just programmed to avoid failure or rejection. What if we could step into something, being completely assured we'll succeed? How would that change your confidence and willingness to pursue it? That is the faith you can have when God asks you to step out of your comfort zone and believe for what He's placed on your heart. Don't let the enemy in to create doubts about a victory that's already written in His Book (Psalm 139:16).

> Don't let the enemy create doubts about a victory that's already written in His Book.

So, I say to you what Mark said in the Scripture at the beginning of this chapter – be watchful. If God placed something on your heart to pray for, do it without hesitation, and then be watchful for the signs of His change, and thankful for how that will bring glory to His kingdom.

Speaking of the enemy, be aware things may not always look the way you think they should. There will be times when things look different or incomplete. For example, if God places on your heart to pray for healing for someone, and that person is only brought partially through their struggle, or even gets worse, don't shrug your shoulders and assume God changed His mind. Instead, expect He's not finished and be watchful. Keep praying, and be excited about how He'll bring it to completion. If God places on your heart to pray for someone you care about to feel fulfilled in their job, and they end up losing it, don't feel confused or doubtful – this might just be God's way of closing the door on the wrong job and bringing that person to the job that will bring them joy. We should never put God in a box. He is a creative type, after all.

Allow your heart to connect with the excitement and enchantment of God at work. Even more amazing, feel the honor and privilege of God allowing you to be a part of it all. Embrace His creativity. Be willing. Be watchful. Believe.

> "Have faith in God," Jesus answered. "Truly I tell you, if anyone says to this mountain, 'Go, throw yourself into the sea,' and does not doubt in their heart but believes that what they say will happen, it will be done for them. Therefore I tell you, whatever you ask for in prayer, believe that you have received it, and it will be yours."
> Mark 11:22-24

Revive | The Upper Room

> Suddenly a sound like the blowing of a violent
> wind came from Heaven and filled the
> whole house where they were sitting.
> Acts 2:2

I love this verse, because when I'm in the waiting room, I refer to what I'm praying for as my "suddenly." We all need spiritual eyes to see the things God is working in the spiritual realm. We would marvel together at the complete control, and the assurance of His hands ushering in our "suddenly." He will usher in our promise at the proper time. Today, I want to take a look at something experienced by the apostles in Acts, Chapter 2. Truly, this is a marvelous example of the promises spoken to our hearts, and of the glorious and faithful ways in which God brings them to pass.

After His death and resurrection, Jesus spent forty days with the apostles, teaching them about the Kingdom of God. On the fortieth day after the Sabbath of Passover week, we learn from Acts Chapter 1 that Jesus was taken up to Heaven. Before He ascended, He gave the apostles an important command. He said, "Do not leave Jerusalem, but wait for the gift My Father promised, which you have heard Me speak about. For John baptized you with water, but in a few days you will be baptized with the Holy Spirit." (Acts 1:4-5). Here, from the very mouth of the living Lord, the apostles are given a promise to receive a gift from God. Jesus told them to wait for it. These words could have been implied, but I believe Christ uses these words to remind us and minister to our hearts today.

There are many times when God speaks something to our hearts with no clear indication of when He will bring it to pass. However, there are times when God gives us a clear timeline in which we can expect Him. Our example today is one of those times. Jesus said clearly in Acts 1:5 the apostles would receive this promised gift "in a few days." One would consider this to be two to three days. However, we learn from Scripture this promise was delivered on the fiftieth day after the Sabbath of Passover week – that is ten days after Jesus spoke those words. As I read and studied this, I had to wonder what the apostles experienced during their wait, and if they struggled in any way to keep the faith on day four, eight, or even the morning of day ten.

Pause with me for a moment while we consider the atmosphere in that upper room. After the apostles processed what they just experienced, I have no doubt they convened in the upper room and, amidst the grief and loss they felt, shared a time of brilliant excitement with each other, musing over what this promise could be. Scripture tells us in Acts 1:14 that those who gathered were in constant prayer. I imagine there were times of silence when all were quietly seeking God, and times of fervor and passion that raised the roof. In all of this, their minds had to be going a million miles per hour. Not only

The Waiting Room

had they just seen their Lord physically ascend into the heavens, but they were waiting in great anticipation for what God promised – something their Lord told them would allow them to do greater things than He (John 14:11-13). I'm certain there were times when one or more of them had a fleeting thought of doubt or grappled with fear or anxiety. Could their wait be filled with any more heightened emotion? I'm sure they battled the same anxieties you face in your own situation today. Their key rested in the words spoken by Christ – to wait for God. This is God's direction for you today. In all things, you are to wait for Him.

The apostles were not disappointed. The Bible tells us on the day of Pentecost, there was a sound like the blowing of a violent wind. The Spirit of the Lord filled the place they were in and rested on each of them in the form of tongues of fire (Acts 2:4). In that moment, they were all filled with a very real and manifest promise of God – the indwelling of the Holy Spirit, alive in each of them. Can you imagine what the apostles must have felt while experiencing their "suddenly?" Can you imagine the absolute joy and awe they must have been feeling? Day ten to the apostles can well represent the final days of your own wait. You can be tired and even discouraged, but when God shows up in a way you can experience, there's no question it's Him, and it will certainly be worth waiting for.

> **When God shows up in a way you can experience, there's no question it's Him, and it will certainly be worth waiting for.**

God created the greatest book ever written. Within that book, He wrote the greatest and truest stories ever told. Can you see the smile on your Father's face when I tell you He loves an exciting ending? He's already written the climax of your "suddenly." Believe for it. When you wait on Him and allow Him to move in His timing, it will be nothing short of spectacular.

> We want each of you to show this same diligence to the very end, in order to make your hope sure. We do not want you to become lazy, but to imitate those who through faith and patience inherit what has been promised.
> Hebrews 6:11-12

The Waiting Room

Revive | Suddenly

> I foretold the former things long ago,
> My mouth announced them and I made
> them known; then suddenly I acted,
> and they came to pass.
> Isaiah 48:3

I hope this Scripture stirs you as deeply as it does me. God is talking to His beloved Israel. He told them what would come to pass before any of it happened, and how He suddenly brought it about. This speaks of a God who is in total and complete control. It speaks of a God of hope and of life. Put aside all your troubles, all your worries, all your anxieties, and ask God to open the eyes of your heart to receive the message He has for you today. It's certainly an exciting one.

A sudden move of God is always preceded by ongoing acts of His hands. What feels like a wait to us is just a spiritual blindness to the flurry of activity God is performing right in front of us. To a baby in utero, what they experience is life and reality to them. Once birthed, their eyes are opened to a world just as real, but much more significant. We live in the earthly realm made

> **A sudden move of God is always preceded by ongoing acts of His hands.**

up only of what we see, hear, taste, smell, and touch. Just as life outside the mother's womb, a spiritual realm exists that holds the true reality. When we are birthed into eternity, our eyes will be opened to that spiritual realm, and we'll see God and the works of His hands in a way none of us could fathom. This is significant because it lays the foundation for why you can continuously seek and place your hope in a God whose control spans not only the spiritual realm, but the earthly as well. Don't look to what you see in this world, but through eyes of faith, to believe what God is doing in the realm unseen. Hold on to your hope. God is faithful.

When God brought this Scripture to me, I felt an excitement well up in my spirit as I read it, and knew He was speaking to my heart. At the time, I had no idea why I felt so excited or what it could mean, but I wrote the Scripture out in my notebook, underlined the word *suddenly* and basked in the strange giddiness that infiltrated my heart. Since that time, He's been faithful to open my eyes to its meaning, but hindsight is always 20/20, isn't it?

Maybe it doesn't have to be. We know our Father's voice (John 10), and we know our Father. The entire Bible is a character description of a God who can be trusted to do what He said He was going to do. The same God who placed every star in its place is the same God at work on *your* "suddenly." If He speaks something to your heart, and you're struggling with doubt, do what King David did when facing a challenge. Think on all the times in the past

> **The same God who placed every star in its place is the same God at work on *your* "suddenly."**

The Waiting Room

when God came through for you. If you're new to your faith and don't have a lot of experiences to draw from yet, then dive into God's Word and pore over the countless examples of how God performed powerful miracles and delivered on incredible promises. Even though these things happened in the past, the God you serve is the same yesterday, today, and forever (Hebrews 13:8). Use that to fuel your expectation. In the process, you'll find it produces joy instead of worry.

What's your "suddenly?" What has your attitude been in the wait? If it's been a struggle, I encourage you to set aside the distractions of this world and immerse yourself in His Word. Study the characteristics of God. In doing so, you'll find your hope is secure in a God whose ways are perfect, whose plans are complete, and whose heart beats to love yours. Like the single flower bud in April, so are God's signs and wonders to those who have eyes to see and ears to hear (Matthew 13:16). In an instant, those flower buds turn into incredible and beautiful flowers in bloom. Lift your eyes to the heavens and know where your help comes from (Psalm 121:1-2). Expect Him. Your "suddenly" is on its way.

> I lift up my eyes to the hills – where does my help come from? My help comes from the Lord, the Maker of heaven and earth. He will not let your foot slip – He who watches over you will not slumber; indeed, He who watches over Israel will neither slumber nor sleep. The Lord watches over you – the Lord is your shade

Caroline Klug

at your right hand; the sun will not harm you by day, nor the moon by night. The Lord will keep you from all harm – He will watch over your life; the Lord will watch over your coming and going both now and forevermore.
Psalm 121:1-8

The Waiting Room

Revive | Ten Years

> The LORD said, "Go out and stand on the mountain in the presence of the LORD, for the LORD is about to pass by." Then a great and powerful wind tore the mountains apart and shattered the rocks before the LORD, but the LORD was not in the winds. After the wind there was an earthquake, but the LORD was not in the earthquake. After the earthquake came a fire, but the LORD was not in the fire. And after the fire came a gentle whisper. When Elijah heard it, he pulled his cloak over his face and went out and stood at the mouth of the cave.
> 1 Kings 19:11-13

It was 2005 when I sat on the edge of the couch, staring down in disbelief. I could see the stack of legal papers on the coffee table, but I wasn't ready to process what was happening. Just two weeks earlier, I had cried out to God over my broken marriage. Not my first. My second. My first marriage ended from infidelity when I was only twenty-six. Now, I was thirty years old, and had spent the last three years living more alone than not, while I prayed against the worldly things my second husband struggled with. It was at that point he had moved in with someone else, and I found myself ready to accept whatever path God wanted me on. I was determined to stay in this and pray my way through for as long as He wanted me to but, if I were to be served divorce papers, I would sign them.

Two weeks later, there they were, lying coldly out on the table in front of me. I found myself in a strange situation. It was like time stopped for a moment to allow me to contemplate my choices. It was before any tears. It was before I had the chance to even react. It was simply quiet and calm, and God's voice brushed past my cheek like a cool breeze. I didn't hear Him audibly, but in only a second, He laid out two choices in front of me. He said, "You can fall apart and let this break you, or you can get on your knees and praise Me in your storm." The moment of strength I found can only be explained by grace. I slid off the couch and onto my knees. I had the Christian radio station on at the time, and a song began playing that will forever be burned in my heart – "Praise You in This Storm," by Casting Crowns. I lifted my hands. I sang. I cried. I even laughed. What He said next would both haunt and bless me in the years to come.

"Ten years." That's what God said. Like our beginning Scripture, it was like a gentle whisper. Ten years. That's all He said. My heart longed for a true partner – one who loved Him as much as I did. My heart knew what He was saying. He was saying it would be ten years until He blessed me with my forever husband. Amidst my pain, I wasn't ready to process that either. Ten years. That's a long time. More time than I wanted to accept so, rather than thank Him, I started trying to figure out what God *really* meant, because it couldn't possibly

The Waiting Room

be ten years from *now*. Maybe He meant ten years from when I first got married. Or maybe He meant ten years from when I lost my dad in college and life got really painful. I twisted that statement around and around my little pea brain until I had God down to delivering a husband in just a few years. See what I did there? I completely missed the blessing and privilege of getting an answer because I was so focused on how long I'd have to wait for it.

> **Don't miss the blessing of getting a *when* because you're too focused on how long you'll have to wait.**

Waiting is uncomfortable, and most of us like to avoid it at all costs.

This would be the length of a book if I went into all the things that happened in the ten years that followed. To give you the CliffsNotes, I made a lot of great decisions, and I made a lot of bad decisions. On the good side, I embraced my faith, the healing, and the teaching. I led a women's ministry, started my own nonprofit organization, blogged, spoke at women's retreats and dreamed of doing big things for God. On the not-so-good side, I got angry that my promise was taking so long. I had immature spiritual temper tantrums wondering why I was doing all this for God and He wasn't doing anything in return. The optimal word there being *immature*. Because of that, I fell onto a broken path for a time. I walked away from ministry, I stopped writing, and I spent time in relationships that were unhealthy. In hindsight, I really feel like I was trying to get fired from my calling. To be honest with you, I was scared of it. Intimidated by it. I felt flawed. But that's because I *was* flawed.

Caroline Klug

For years, I felt Him calling. For years, I felt Him wooing me back. My heart longed for Him, but the guilt of my choices kept me estranged. It wasn't until the spring of 2015 when I'd had enough. My heart was broken and so was my spirit. I didn't want the emptiness anymore. I wanted Him. The problem was, my heart was still hard. I found my way to a Christian counselor I had seen a decade earlier. I knew it had to be her. My heart was hard, but I felt God leading me to her because she would tell me the truth. She did. I only went a few times before I got too angry again, but her words were what I needed to eventually bring the wall down. I was broken, but in a different way. In a good way. In a forgiven way. There's nothing quite like the feeling of recognizing a new start after knowing where you were. I committed to doing things His way. Not my way anymore. His way or the highway, as they say, and I was faithful to that.

Three months later I met Jim, my now forever husband. Little did I know, at the time, Jim had made a similar commitment just before meeting me, to give his search completely over to God. Another coincidence? I think not. God knows exactly what He's doing. Exactly. I love that we first met on August 18th, the anniversary of when I first gave my life to Christ. I find it no coincidence that I met the two most important men in my life on the same day. Speaking of no coincidence, it wasn't until after Jim and I were engaged in the fall of 2016 that the words I had buried so deeply for so long came floating past my cheek once more like that cool and familiar breeze. "Ten years." Tears welled up in my eyes and I felt completely humbled by the awareness of a promise fulfilled. He who promised was faithful indeed (Hebrews 10:23).

Today, I'm married to the partner I prayed an ocean of tears for. Was it worth the wait? Yes. Without a doubt. It was a difficult ten years. Mostly because I made it difficult. But He was with me the whole time. He's with you, too. Through all of your successes and failures. Through all of your joy and grief. He's there. He has a plan. He knows the choices you'll make, He knows the choices others will make, and He's in complete control. Don't lose heart. Keep seeking Him.

> **God knows the exact date and time of your "suddenly."**

God knows the exact date and time of your "suddenly."

■ I remain confident of this: I will see the goodness of the LORD in the land of the living. Wait for the LORD; be strong and take heart and wait for the LORD. Psalm 27:13-14

Caroline Klug

Parting Thoughts

I pray what you've read on these pages has blessed you, ministered to your heart, and encouraged you to keep a right perspective during your wait. I'd like to wrap up our time together by sharing a beautiful verse that touches me deeply, along with an insight God has used to bless me over and over again:

Take delight in the LORD, and He will give you the desires of your heart (Psalm 37:4).

I'm pretty sure my heart swells a few sizes when I read this verse. Kind of like that scene in *How the Grinch Stole Christmas*, when we see the heart of the Grinch grow several sizes larger. I like that example, because I can kind of relate to the Grinch. His heart didn't swell until he finally understood the true meaning of Christmas. Mine didn't swell until I finally understood the true meaning of this verse, which was after I made a few laps around the desert.

I used to think it meant if I was being a good Christian and doing all the things good Christians were supposed to do, that God would reward that good behavior by giving me the stuff I prayed for. At first, I was disappointed when I found out that was wrong. I would even go so far as to say I got a little defensive when someone explained to me that God wasn't giving me *my* desires. God was giving me *His* desires. My first, very immature thought was, "Well, that doesn't sound like as much fun." Oh, how wrong I was.

I can only pray I can do this next part justice. In fact, I'm going to pause for a moment to pray before I write this out, because I *really* want you to get this.

When you give God all that you are, which includes all your dreams, desires, needs, fears, and expectations, and when you make Him the very thing you delight over above all else, then He will shape the desires He knows are perfectly suited to you and plant them deep within your heart. When this happens, it's no longer us desiring the things we think are good. It's us desiring the things God knows is best. Something magical happens here that I don't want you to miss. And when I say magical, I mean supernatural.

You might have something very specific that is the single biggest desire of your heart. When you make God your single biggest desire, you're allowing Him to take that dream and mold it in His hands. What He plants back inside of you may look a little different, but you'll find that you desire His version more than yours. The magical part is, His passions are now your passions, and your hearts are perfectly aligned. When God places something in your heart, it's a sure thing. By giving your dreams and prayers over to God, you lose nothing. But you gain everything.

I would be remiss if I didn't call out something wonderful about this verse. The Hebrew translation behind the word delight, which is *ânag*, implies one of the meanings to be figuratively pliable. In order for God to place something in our hearts, it requires our hearts to first be pliable enough to work with it. What great imagery God gave to us.

You might still be in the waiting room, but you have an opportunity to turn your wonder into wonderment. Have a mindset of awe over what you believe He can do and respect for His greater plan at work. Be excited about what He's going to do in you, through you and for you.

Watch for Him. Expect Him. Delight in Him, and He will give you the desires of your heart.

Caroline Klug

Scripture References

* References where entire chapters are mentioned will not be expanded.

Personal Message:
1. Psalm 121:4 – indeed, He who watches over Israel will neither slumber nor sleep.
2. Psalm 139:4 – Before a word is on my tongue You, Lord, know it completely.

First Things First:
1. Genesis 15, 21
2. Exodus 16
3. Joshua 1
4. Daniel 3
5. Daniel 6
6. Hebrews 13:8 – Jesus Christ is the same yesterday and today and forever.
7. 2 Chronicles 20
8. Ephesians 3:20 – Now to Him who is able to do immeasurably more than all we ask or imagine, according to His power that is at work within us...

Step 1: Remind Your Heart:
1. Exodus
2. Romans 8:28 – And we know that in all things God works for the good of those who love Him, who have been called according to His purpose.

Caroline Klug

Remind | Labor Pains:
1. Psalm 139:16 – Your eyes saw my unformed body; all the days ordained for me were written in Your book before one of them came to be.

Remind | Impatience:
1. Matthew 10:30 – And even the very hairs of your head are all numbered.
2. Isaiah 50:7 – Because the Sovereign Lord helps me, I will not be disgraced. Therefore have I set my face like flint, and I know I will not be put to shame.
3. Romans 8:28 – And we know that in all things God works for the good of those who love Him, who have been called according to His purpose.
4. Luke 6:45 – A good man brings good things out of the good stored up in his heart, and an evil man brings evil things out of the evil stored up in his heart. For the mouth speaks what the heart is full of.
5. Matthew 19:26 – Jesus looked at them and said, "With man this is impossible, but with God all things are possible."
6. Psalm 27:13 – I remain confident of this: I will see the goodness of the Lord in the land of the living.
7. Ephesians 1:23 – ...which is His body, the fullness of Him who fills everything in every way.

Remind | The Wait (Part 1):
1. Galatians 5:16-17 – So I say, walk by the Spirit, and you will not gratify the desires of the flesh. For the flesh desires what is contrary to the Spirit, and the Spirit what is contrary to the flesh. They are in conflict with each other, so that you are not to do whatever you want.
2. Proverbs 16:9 – In their hearts humans plan their course, but the Lord establishes their steps.
3. Ephesians 1:9-10 – He made known to us the mystery of His will according to his good pleasure, which He

The Waiting Room

purposed in Christ, to be put into effect when the times reach their fulfillment—to bring unity to all things in heaven and on earth under Christ.
4. Genesis 12
5. Genesis 15-17

Remind | The Wait (Part 2):
1. Hebrews 12:2 – ...fixing our eyes on Jesus, the pioneer and perfecter of faith. For the joy set before Him He endured the cross, scorning its shame, and sat down at the right hand of the throne of God.
2. Mark 12:30 – Love the Lord your God with all your heart and with all your soul and with all your mind and with all your strength.
3. Matthew 28:18-20 – Then Jesus came to them and said, "All authority in heaven and on earth has been given to Me. Therefore go and make disciples of all nations, baptizing them in the name of the Father and of the Son and of the Holy Spirit, and teaching them to obey everything I have commanded you. And surely I am with you always, to the very end of the age."
4. 2 Timothy 1:7 – For the Spirit God gave us does not make us timid, but gives us power, love and self-discipline.
5. Luke 12:7 – Indeed, the very hairs of your head are all numbered. Don't be afraid; you are worth more than many sparrows.
6. Psalm 13:1-6 – How long, Lord? Will You forget me forever? How long will You hide Your face from me? How long must I wrestle with my thoughts and day after day have sorrow in my heart? How long will my enemy triumph over me? Look on me and answer, Lord my God. Give light to my eyes, or I will sleep in death, and my enemy will say, "I have overcome him," and my foes will rejoice when I fall. But I trust in Your unfailing love; my

heart rejoices in Your salvation. I will sing the Lord's praise, for He has been good to me.

Remind | When, God, When?:
1. 1 Corinthians 12:8-10 – To one there is given through the Spirit a message of wisdom, to another a message of knowledge by means of the same Spirit, to another faith by the same Spirit, to another gifts of healing by that one Spirit, to another miraculous powers, to another prophecy, to another distinguishing between spirits, to another speaking in different kinds of tongues, and to still another the interpretation of tongues.
2. 1 Corinthians 12:27-28 – Now you are the body of Christ, and each one of you is a part of it. And God has placed in the church first of all apostles, second prophets, third teachers, then miracles, then gifts of healing, of helping, of guidance, and of different kinds of tongues.

Remind | War of Wills:
1. Proverbs 3:5-6 – Trust in the Lord with all your heart and lean not on your own understanding; in all your ways submit to Him, and He will make your paths straight.
2. Philippians 3:7-9 – But whatever were gains to me I now consider loss for the sake of Christ. What is more, I consider everything a loss because of the surpassing worth of knowing Christ Jesus my Lord, for whose sake I have lost all things. I consider them garbage, that I may gain Christ and be found in Him, not having a righteousness of my own that comes from the law, but that which is through faith in Christ—the righteousness that comes from God on the basis of faith.
2. Psalm 139:16 – Your eyes saw my unformed body; all the days ordained for me were written in Your book before one of them came to be.

The Waiting Room

3. Ephesians 6:12 – For our struggle is not against flesh and blood, but against the rulers, against the authorities, against the powers of this dark world and against the spiritual forces of evil in the heavenly realms.
4. Ephesians 6:17 – Take the helmet of salvation and the sword of the Spirit, which is the word of God.
5. Hebrews 4:12 – For the word of God is alive and active. Sharper than any double-edged sword, it penetrates even to dividing soul and spirit, joints and marrow; it judges the thoughts and attitudes of the heart.
6. Philippians 4:7 – And the peace of God, which transcends all understanding, will guard your hearts and your minds in Christ Jesus.

Remind | Walk by Faith:
1. Ephesians 3:20 – Now to Him who is able to do immeasurably more than all we ask or imagine, according to His power that is at work within us...
2. Romans 8:31 – What, then, shall we say in response to these things? If God is for us, who can be against us?
3. 1 Peter 4:11 – If anyone speaks, they should do so as one who speaks the very words of God. If anyone serves, they should do so with the strength God provides, so that in all things God may be praised through Jesus Christ. To Him be the glory and the power for ever and ever. Amen.

Remind | The Peace of God:
1. Exodus 14:13 – Moses answered the people, "Do not be afraid. Stand firm and you will see the deliverance the Lord will bring you today. The Egyptians you see today you will never see again."
2. John 11: 41-42 – So they took away the stone. Then Jesus looked up and said, "Father, I thank You that You have heard Me. I knew that You always hear Me, but I said this

for the benefit of the people standing here, that they may believe that You sent Me."
3. Romans 8:28 – And we know that in all things God works for the good of those who love Him, who have been called according to His purpose.

Remind | Milk and Honey:
1. Psalm 139:13 – Were I to count them, they would outnumber the grains of sand—when I awake, I am still with you.
2. 1 John 4:8 – Whoever does not love does not know God, because God is love.
3. Joshua 1

Step 2: Release Your Heart:
1. Hebrews 13:8 – Jesus Christ is the same yesterday and today and forever.
2. 1 John 4:7-8 – Dear friends, let us love one another, for love comes from God. Everyone who loves has been born of God and knows God. Whoever does not love does not know God, because God is love.

Release | Letting Go:
1. Psalm 37:24 – though he may stumble, he will not fall, for the Lord upholds him with his hand.

Release | A New Thing (Part 1):
1. Psalm 103:12 – ...as far as the east is from the west, so far has He removed our transgressions from us.
2. John 7:38 – Whoever believes in Me, as Scripture has said, rivers of living water will flow from within them.
3. Matthew 7:16-17 – By their fruit you will recognize them. Do people pick grapes from thornbushes, or figs from thistles? Likewise, every good tree bears good fruit, but a bad tree bears bad fruit.

The Waiting Room

Release | A New Thing (Part 2):
1. 2 Corinthians 4:18 – So we fix our eyes not on what is seen, but on what is unseen, since what is seen is temporary, but what is unseen is eternal.
2. 1 Peter 5:6 – Humble yourselves, therefore, under God's mighty hand, that He may lift you up in due time.
3. Psalm 145:15 – The eyes of all look to You, and You give them their food at the proper time.
4. Ephesians 6:13 – Therefore put on the full armor of God, so that when the day of evil comes, you may be able to stand your ground, and after you have done everything, to stand.

Release | Lift Up Your Eyes:
1. Jeremiah 29:11 – "For I know the plans I have for you," declares the Lord, "plans to prosper you and not to harm you, plans to give you hope and a future."
2. Philippians 1:6 – ...being confident of this, that He who began a good work in you will carry it on to completion until the day of Christ Jesus.

Release | Spring of Life (Part 1):
1. Jeremiah 2:13 – My people have committed two sins: They have forsaken me, the spring of living water, and have dug their own cisterns, broken cisterns that cannot hold water.
2. John 7:38 – Whoever believes in Me, as Scripture has said, rivers of living water will flow from within them.
3. 1 Corinthians 2:2 – For I resolved to know nothing while I was with you except Jesus Christ and Him crucified.
4. John 4

Release | The Call to Persevere:
1. Job 1:7 – The Lord said to Satan, "Where have you come from?" Satan answered the Lord, "From roaming throughout the earth, going back and forth on it."

2. 1 Peter 5:8 – Be alert and of sober mind. Your enemy the devil prowls around like a roaring lion looking for someone to devour.
3. 1 Peter 1:3-7 – Praise be to the God and Father of our Lord Jesus Christ! In His great mercy He has given us new birth into a living hope through the resurrection of Jesus Christ from the dead, and into an inheritance that can never perish, spoil or fade. This inheritance is kept in heaven for you, who through faith are shielded by God's power until the coming of the salvation that is ready to be revealed in the last time. In all this you greatly rejoice, though now for a little while you may have had to suffer grief in all kinds of trials. These have come so that the proven genuineness of your faith—of greater worth than gold, which perishes even though refined by fire—may result in praise, glory and honor when Jesus Christ is revealed.
4. Romans 8:28 – And we know that in all things God works for the good of those who love Him, who have been called according to His purpose.

Release | The Climb Upward:
1. Exodus 3-4
2. Exodus 3:5 – "Do not come any closer," God said. "Take off your sandals, for the place where you are standing is holy ground."
3. John 10:10 – The thief comes only to steal and kill and destroy; I have come that they may have life, and have it to the full.

Release | Surrender:
3. Psalm 139:16 – Your eyes saw my unformed body; all the days ordained for me were written in Your book before one of them came to be.

The Waiting Room

1. John 10:10 – The thief comes only to steal and kill and destroy; I have come that they may have life, and have it to the full.
2. 2 Timothy 1:7 – For the Spirit God gave us does not make us timid, but gives us power, love and self-discipline.
3. Ephesians 3:17-19 – ...so that Christ may dwell in your hearts through faith. And I pray that you, being rooted and established in love, may have power, together with all the Lord's holy people, to grasp how wide and long and high and deep is the love of Christ, and to know this love that surpasses knowledge—that you may be filled to the measure of all the fullness of God.
4. 1 John 4:8 – Whoever does not love does not know God, because God is love.
5. Psalm 37:4 – Take delight in the Lord, and He will give you the desires of your heart.
6. Matthew 7:9-11 – Which of you, if your son asks for bread, will give him a stone? Or if he asks for a fish, will give him a snake? If you, then, though you are evil, know how to give good gifts to your children, how much more will your Father in heaven give good gifts to those who ask Him!

Release | Cut the Ropes:
1. Acts 27:21 – After they had gone a long time without food, Paul stood up before them and said: "Men, you should have taken my advice not to sail from Crete; then you would have spared yourselves this damage and loss."
2. Acts 27:22-25 – But now I urge you to keep up your courage, because not one of you will be lost; only the ship will be destroyed. Last night an angel of the God to whom I belong and whom I serve stood beside me and said, "Do not be afraid, Paul. You must stand trial before Caesar; and God has graciously given you the lives of all who sail with you." So keep up your courage, men, for I have faith in God that it will happen just as He told me.

3. Acts 27:32 – So the soldiers cut the ropes that held the lifeboat and let it drift away.

Step 3: Revive Your Heart:
1. Romans 8:28 – And we know that in all things God works for the good of those who love Him, who have been called according to His purpose.
2. Psalm 30:11-12 – You turned my wailing into dancing; You removed my sackcloth and clothed me with joy, that my heart may sing Your praises and not be silent. Lord my God, I will praise You forever.
3. Genesis 15:5 – He took him outside and said, "Look up at the sky and count the stars—if indeed you can count them." Then He said to him, "So shall your offspring be."
4. Romans 4:18-21 – Against all hope, Abraham in hope believed and so became the father of many nations, just as it had been said to him, "So shall your offspring be." Without weakening in his faith, he faced the fact that his body was as good as dead—since he was about a hundred years old—and that Sarah's womb was also dead. Yet he did not waver through unbelief regarding the promise of God, but was strengthened in his faith and gave glory to God, being fully persuaded that God had power to do what He had promised.
5. Hebrews 13:8 – Jesus Christ is the same yesterday and today and forever.
6. Joshua 24:15 – But if serving the Lord seems undesirable to you, then choose for yourselves this day whom you will serve, whether the gods your ancestors served beyond the Euphrates, or the gods of the Amorites, in whose land you are living. But as for me and my household, we will serve the Lord."

The Waiting Room

Revive | Great Expectations:
1. Mark 9:23 – "If you can?" said Jesus. "Everything is possible for one who believes."

Revive | Dry Bones (Part 1):
1. John 16:33 – I have told you these things, so that in me you may have peace. In this world you will have trouble. But take heart! I have overcome the world.

Revive | Let Nothing Move You:
1. 2 Chronicles 20:15 – He said: "Listen, King Jehoshaphat and all who live in Judah and Jerusalem! This is what the Lord says to you: 'Do not be afraid or discouraged because of this vast army. For the battle is not yours, but God's.
2. 1 Corinthians 10:13 – No temptation has overtaken you except what is common to mankind. And God is faithful; He will not let you be tempted beyond what you can bear. But when you are tempted, He will also provide a way out so that you can endure it.
5. Ephesians 6:13 – Therefore put on the full armor of God, so that when the day of evil comes, you may be able to stand your ground, and after you have done everything, to stand.

Revive | Set Your Mind:
1. Daniel 10:12-14 – Then he continued, "Do not be afraid, Daniel. Since the first day that you set your mind to gain understanding and to humble yourself before your God, your words were heard, and I have come in response to them. But the prince of the Persian kingdom resisted me twenty-one days. Then Michael, one of the chief princes, came to help me, because I was detained there with the king of Persia. Now I have come to explain to you what will happen to your people in the future, for the vision concerns a time yet to come."

2. Ephesians 6:17 – Take the helmet of salvation and the sword of the Spirit, which is the word of God.

Revive | Be Watchful:
1. Isaiah 40:26 – Lift up your eyes and look to the heavens: Who created all these? He who brings out the starry host one by one and calls forth each of them by name. Because of His great power and mighty strength, not one of them is missing.
2. Psalm 147:4 – He determines the number of the stars and calls them each by name.
4. Psalm 139:16 – Your eyes saw my unformed body; all the days ordained for me were written in Your book before one of them came to be.
3. John 16:33 – I have told you these things, so that in Me you may have peace. In this world you will have trouble. But take heart! I have overcome the world.

Revive | The Upper Room:
1. Acts 1
2. Acts 1:4-5 – On one occasion, while He was eating with them, He gave them this command: "Do not leave Jerusalem, but wait for the gift My Father promised, which you have heard Me speak about. For John baptized with water, but in a few days you will be baptized with the Holy Spirit."
3. John 14:11-13 – Believe Me when I say that I am in the Father and the Father is in Me; or at least believe on the evidence of the works themselves. Very truly I tell you, whoever believes in Me will do the works I have been doing, and they will do even greater things than these, because I am going to the Father. And I will do whatever you ask in My name, so that the Father may be glorified in the Son.

The Waiting Room

4. Acts 2:4 – All of them were filled with the Holy Spirit and began to speak in other tongues as the Spirit enabled them.

Revive | Suddenly:
1. John 10
2. Hebrews 13:8 – Jesus Christ is the same yesterday and today and forever.
3. Matthew 13:16 – But blessed are your eyes because they see, and your ears because they hear.
4. Psalm 121:1-2 – I lift up my eyes to the mountains—where does my help come from? My help comes from the Lord, the Maker of heaven and earth.

Revive | Ten Years:
1. Hebrews 10:23 – Let us hold unswervingly to the hope we profess, for He who promised is faithful.

Parting Thoughts:
1. Psalm 37:4 – Take delight in the Lord, and He will give you the desires of your heart.

Caroline Klug

Stolen
By Caroline Klug

Stolen is more than a fiction thriller. It's a biblical allegory about redemption. Available on Amazon and Barnes & Noble.

Seventeen and on the streets, Star is a runaway headed down a dark path. It becomes even darker when she catches the eye of a serial killer who holds her captive in a remote prison in the woods. Failed escapes, physical torture, and mental anguish mark her days in isolation.

Alternating chapters weave her story around Sarah, a woman riddled with questions about her own past, who suspects the man she lives with may not be what he seems. As the stories unfold and connect, perhaps there's a twist that will make you want to go back and read it again.

This story brings to life the anguish of isolation and the choices that paved the way into their prisons. It also brings the gentle whisper of love and the audacious hope of freedom. Stolen is a thriller that will take the reader on a journey of pain and terror, as well as an unexpected journey of redemption.

Caroline Klug is an author of inspirational fiction, using thrillers and short story collections as a way to bring insights to people all over the world.

In addition to fiction, Caroline writes Christian Living books that teach, inspire and encourage.

To see other books by this author visit:
www.CarolineKlug.com

Caroline Klug

www.ingramcontent.com/pod-product-compliance
Lightning Source LLC
Chambersburg PA
CBHW020414080526
44584CB00014B/1331